This Is Not a Love Story

Also by Judy Brown

Hush

(written under the pseudonym Eishes Chayil)

This Is Not a Love Story

A Memoir

Judy Brown

Little, Brown and Company

New York Boston London

Little, Brown and Company
Hachette Book Group
1290 Avenue of the Americas, New York, NY 10104
littlebrown.com

First Edition: July 2015

Little, Brown and Company is a division of Hachette Book Group, Inc. The Little, Brown name and logo are trademarks of Hachette Book Group, Inc.

The publisher is not responsible for websites (or their content) that are not owned by the publisher.

The Hachette Speakers Bureau provides a wide range of authors for speaking events. To find out more, go to hachettespeakersbureau.com or call (866) 376-6591.

ISBN 978-0-316-40072-5
LCCN 2014922208

10 9 8 7 6 5 4 3 2 1

RRD-C

Printed in the United States of America

Author's Note

For the sake of privacy, I have changed all first and last names—including my own and those of my family members—except for Dr. Cory Shulman's. For the sake of clarity, I have left out certain characters. The stories passed on by aunts, uncles, great-aunts, and great-uncles—guardians and messengers of the family history—are all told in the book by one beloved aunt. It is the same with the children: Blimi, my best friend, is a composite of several young friends, all of whom knew or repeated rumors and myths that surrounded the strange mystery that was my brother.

This Is Not a Love Story

Prologue

Once, when I was in third grade, my teacher said that it was forbidden to fall in love. It was God who decided who would marry whom, and only the rebbe knows these secrets.

You see, up above the clouds, by the royal throne, God and his angels are gathered. It is there, forty days before each person is born, that a heavenly voice calls out in the skies, proclaiming, "The daughter of this man and this woman will marry the son of that man and that woman."

Or something like that. It says so in the Talmud.

My teacher also told us about that time long ago when a Roman princess asked a great rebbe, "What has your God been doing ever since he finished creating earth?" And he answered, "Matchmaking." The Roman princess laughed. She said, "I can do that too," and ordered a thousand of her female slaves to be paired up with a thousand of her male slaves that very night. But the next morning, they came to her, all two thousand, with scratches and wounds, crying, "I don't

want to be with him," "I wanted to marry someone else..."
There was chaos in the court.

The Roman princess immediately called the great rebbe.
She said, "Rebbe, every word in your Torah is great. Only
your God is true."

So this book about my family's curse is not a love story.
Because my mother and father never fell in love. That would
have been a terrible sin, a gentile kind of nonsense, and my
parents were pious people. It was my brother who was crazy,
crazy as a bat, and because of him we were cursed. That's
why people told lies about my family, things about love and
such—stories that could never be. It says so in the Talmud:
There is no such thing as love.

Part I

One

September 1988

When I was in third grade, I made a deal with God.

I would fast for forty days and nights, and in return He'd make for me a miracle. Fasting forty days and nights was an ancient custom, a powerful way to get God's attention. All the holy saints of once upon a time did this. They had to when they realized just how stubborn God was, and that there were problems for which prayers were not enough. God wanted suffering.

I needed this ancient omen to work so that Hashem, our one true God, would get me new heart-shaped earrings. I figured if the saints could get Hashem to listen when they asked for rain after a long drought, or for an end to a terrible plague, it would certainly work for me. Earrings were a simple miracle.

The earrings I wanted were pretty, ruby red, with a perfect glow, lying in the window of Gold's jewelry store in Borough Park. I had first seen them two weeks earlier when I went shopping with my mother for a school sweater and school panty hose. I had prayed and prayed for them ever since, but nothing had happened. I'd thrown in extra psalms before bed, yet from Heaven there was only silence.

Then my third grade teacher, Mrs. Friedman, told us the story about the saints and their forty-day fasts during times of drought. She described how on the fortieth day, at the stroke of dawn, as the red streaks of sun rose above the earth and the gaunt, starving face of the tzaddik, it began to rain. Nay, pour. And the people of Israel were saved.

That afternoon, I sat in the big, wooden blanket box attached to the head of my bed and struck a deal with God. I would fast for forty days and nights, and He would get me the earrings.

After a thorough talk, it was agreed. I climbed out of the box.

I began my fast the next morning. I got out of bed, into my school uniform, walked to the kitchen, and pulled the cornflakes from the shelf in the pantry. Then I remembered. I could not eat. I was fasting.

I put the cereal back and went to my room. I sat on my bed and thought. Mostly, I thought of the cereal. I was hungry. I wanted to eat now. I had always known that fasting meant not eating, but I had never connected it with hunger. Somehow the saints just did it. Somehow my mother did not have breakfast, lunch, or supper on Yom Kippur while I ate my snack in the shul yard. But real fasting—this was hard. My stomach was empty, my mouth watered, and my entire being wanted cereal, any cereal.

At school that day, my stomach growled loudly. By recess, I could barely hear my own thoughts—and this was only the first of forty days. Two minutes before the end of recess, I gave up. I could not do this any longer. I crammed an entire bag of pretzels in my mouth. The bell rang. I grabbed my lunch bag. I pushed my tuna sandwich into my mouth and chewed as I hurried back to my classroom. Then Mrs. Friedman walked in, and I sat at my desk, relieved. I now had a clearer focus. I could renegotiate with God.

Mrs. Friedman was teaching us the meaning of the morning prayers.

"Girls," she said briskly, her long skirt brushing by my desk as she walked up and down the aisles, "when we pray to Hashem, we are talking directly with a king, and not just any king, but the one and only king of the universe. The one and only king who can grant any wish in the world. When you stand in the royal court of a king, do you slouch? Do you yawn? Do you stuff banana into your mouth in the middle of the conversation?"

Mrs. Friedman stood still. She towered over my best friend, Blimi Krieger, who slouched behind her desk in the first row. Blimi was holding a banana peel, the last of the fruit squashed furtively between the cover and the first page of her prayer book. She held the prayer book tightly against her chest, the banana squeezing slowly out the side. It landed with a splat on the floor.

"And do you think," Mrs. Friedman asked, pointedly, "that

the king of the universe likes banana mush squished onto His heavenly prayers?"

Blimi began to cry. Mrs. Friedman handed her paper towels to wipe the mess off her prayers. Then, once more, she walked up and down the aisles, nudging our pointer fingers onto the right line in the holy book.

All this was important, of course, even sacred, perhaps, but I had more urgent matters at hand. This fast wasn't working. I needed different conditions. I needed breakfast.

I told God that I'd still get the ruby earrings, but forsaking cornflakes in a bowl was not part of the deal. To fast, one must have strength, and for strength, one must eat breakfast. I would start fasting each morning right after the cereal.

The next morning, I ate a large bowl of cornflakes with chocolate syrup and sugar. I held the syrup bottle upside down and stuck my tongue into the pouring stream. But my mother, wrapping chocolate-spread sandwiches in foil, said, "Are you crazy? *What* are you doing?" Half a bottle of chocolate syrup, she said, putting the bottle safely out of my reach, was enough for any breakfast.

At recess, I gave my snack away. I gave Blimi my Milk Munch and watched her eat it. She munched on it, crunched on it, licked the caramel cream, and promised to be my closest friend forevermore. I walked around forlornly all recess long. Blimi chatted away, happy as pie.

But then came lunch. God and I had not told my mother about the deal, so she had in ignorance packed me one. And now Blimi was eating her grilled cheese sandwich right in front of my face. My lunch was in the schoolbag under my chair: two slices of white bread with thick chocolate spread just the way I liked it.

Ten minutes before the end of lunch, I ate the sandwich. I ate it quickly, so that I did not really taste the goodness of it. I explained patiently to God that a quick lunch wasn't a real lunch, that it was therefore still allowed in our agreement, and mostly that I was really hungry.

At home that night, I was careful with supper. I ate the chicken, the potato, but not the soup or the vegetables. Then only part of dessert. It was as if I hadn't eaten at all. Even my mother said so. She frowned.. "Look—the soup and vegetables! You haven't eaten anything."

I explained that I could not. There were important considerations, and soup and vegetables were out for the next month.

My mother looked at me suspiciously. She said I had better eat what she put on the table and now. But I said no. I would not give in. This was an important test of faith, I knew. God was peering down at me from between the clouds, and if I ate my vegetables the deal was off. I'd never see the red ruby earrings again.

Just then the phone rang. It was someone from Israel. My mother walked away chatting, the receiver under her ear.

I quickly ran to my room.

I sat in my box, the one attached to my bed. I covered the top with a blanket. I tore the wrapping off the two Peanut Chews I'd hidden. Peanut Chews didn't count. They were part of an agreed-upon break from the fast each day. And since they were hidden in the box, God agreed that, though He was

God, He would nevertheless turn His eyes away and look elsewhere.

I fasted this way for four days. On the fifth, I stopped. I was no longer giving away my chocolate; Blimi was therefore not my best friend. And even vegetables had begun to look good.

Enough, I told Hashem. Four entire days had passed. I was tired of eating Peanut Chews in a box, and if He was God at all, He'd count it as forty. After all, I was only eight, but He— He was the Almighty, the One, True, and Only. And anyway, it was the thought that counted, not what I had eaten.

Two days later, I got new earrings. My father brought them home as a complete surprise, but I knew that Hashem had made him do it. That was the mystery of God. Things happened somehow. The earrings were bow-shaped, not heart-shaped, as I had dreamt, but still. From far away they looked like hearts.

Only four weeks later, I made my second deal with Heaven. But this one, I explained, was really important. More important than the earrings, more important than a new dress, more important than any plague or drought. It was my crazy brother, Nachum. He had come back home, and I needed a miracle now.

From inside my blanket box, I sealed the deal with God. I would fast for forty days and also forty nights, and then, on the dawn of the forty-first, He'd make my crazy brother normal.

Two

I hadn't seen my brother Nachum in more than a year, ever since he had been given away. I was seven years old and he six when it happened, at the end of the summer after first grade. My mother had taken us to Israel for summer vacation, all six of us kids, but when we came back to New York, there were only five. She had left Nachum behind.

Ever since then, things had been good at home, and I saw no reason for this to change. But only a few weeks after starting third grade, I came home from school and Nachum was there, playing Lego on the floor by the door, my mother smiling joyfully behind him.

I gasped and dropped my schoolbag.

My mother's eyes were wide with happiness. "Menuchah!" she said. "Come give your brother a hug!"

So I gave Nachum a hug.

"Tell him that you missed him," she said.

I told Nachum I had missed him.

Nachum giggled to himself. He never said hello. He started playing with the pieces of his Lego set.

"*Nu?*" my mother said. "*Nu?* What do you say? Nachum is home!" She said it as if she had brought home a surprise Chanukah gift, one that I had been waiting for all this time.

I could not believe my eyes. My crazy brother had finally gone away, and now, voluntarily, she had brought him back? Didn't she remember the trouble he had made before, the messes, the noises, the nights she had tied his leg to the bed so he wouldn't wander out of the house? Why was she so happy?

My older sister, Rivky, explained it to me after supper. "Nachum is smarter now," she said. "Ima said he got better."

Rivky was extremely good. She was nine, a year older than I was, and did her homework every day. Then she'd help clean up and take care of my baby brother, Avrumi. I did not trust Rivky, with her clean and trimmed nails and stick-straight dark hair, but my oldest brother, Yitzy, eleven years old and not nearly as clean or saintly, said the same thing. He told me that Nachum was cured now. He could say full sentences and even answer questions. My mother had prayed, the rebbe had blessed, and our brother, crazy as a bat before, was healed.

My father said nothing.

But my father did not speak much anyway. He was a practical man, tall and strong, with a short black beard. Everyone said that my father was as straight as a ruler, always to the point, like the time Aunt Chedvah was sick and everyone prayed and hoped, saying, God will help, surely God will help, except my father, who said, "She'll die this week." He'd been correct. And like the time he said I was prettier than all my friends. And like the time he said, "Something's wrong with the boy. He'll never change."

My father and I liked to play. When he came home from work in the evenings, I'd run to open the door. Then we'd play catch around the glass dining room table.

"I come home," my father would say, laughing, "end you dun' even give me vuhn kees?"

That's how my father spoke English, in a thick, funny accent, saying "kees" instead of "kiss," and "eh" for "ah." At home we spoke mainly Hebrew, the language of Israel, the country both of my parents had grown up in. Sometimes I spoke English with my father, but no matter how many times I practiced with him, saying, "Kiss. K-*iiih-s. Kiss!*," he said, "K*ee*s."

"No!" I would shout. "I am not giving you any k*ee*ses!"

I kissed my father every day. I'd jump on him, he'd lift me up high, and I would put my arms around his neck. But my father's beard was itchy, it scratched my cheek, so the day Nachum came home, I said no. There were no more free kisses. I wanted payment.

My father chuckled. He laid a chair on the floor sideways between the door and the glass table, blocking my escape.

"Uh-kay," he said. "How much you vant? How much?"

I jumped excitedly. "A hundred! I want a hundred!"

"Nuh problem," he declared. "I give you vuhn hundred."

I knew that trick.

"Not one hundred kisses! One hundred dollars!"

My father sprinted around the table. "Nuh vay! I give you vuhn hundred keeses!"

Shrieking happily, I fled the dining room, running down the narrow hallway. I rushed toward the bathroom at the end of the hall to hide, but Nachum's bedroom was right in between, and he came out just as I passed by. I swerved wildly around him, my elbow brushing him roughly.

Nachum froze.

Then he screamed. "Eeeeeeeeee!"

He threw his hands up, as if pushing bees away. He blinked frantically, squinting as though he was staring into the noon sun. Then he froze again.

My father walked up the hall, straight and fast like a soldier, and leaned over my brother. He lifted up Nachum's chin. "What happened?" he asked in Hebrew. "What happened, Nachum? What happened?"

Nachum did not look up. He pushed his head down and to the side, his eyes reaching for the emptiness behind my father, at the dark end of the hallway.

"Nachum?"

My brother moved quickly, walking hurriedly to the empty space. My father looked after him. His eyes darkened. I bounced up and down, waving my hands.

"Abba, Abba, you can't catch me! Catch me, catch me!"

But my father was watching Nachum. The twinkle in his eyes was gone. He did not play catch with me again that evening.

My mother was tall and strong too. Her wig, a bright copper red, was the color of her real hair, and when she spoke, her voice was commanding. During the week, in the early mornings, my mother taught in the ultraorthodox girls' high school, and once, during a school holiday party, three of her students gathered around me, leaning over, and asked furtively, "Are you very scared of your mother?"

Everyone said I looked like my mother, but I did not. My eyes were hazel like hers, it's true, but they never blazed the way hers did when she meant business, no matter how much I practiced in the mirror. And though I'd colored my hair with a bright red marker, the color had washed right off in the bath, leaving me with plain brown. Maybe I looked like my mother, but in a short and bland version, with buck teeth, and cheeks that were chubby and round while my mother's cheekbones were high and firm.

Nachum looked like neither of my parents. He just looked like himself. One afternoon, a neighbor watching him run like the wind down the block called him a beautiful child. She said he had a perfect heart-shaped face, and pretty, curving eyes. She thought the freckles scattered over his face were adorable, and those two dimples that appeared when he smiled—just so cute.

I didn't see the pretty in Nachum no matter which way I looked at him, and I looked closely at my brother all that first week after his return to check if he was cured.

But Nachum wasn't cured. He still blinked his eyes as though there were pebbles in them. I knew because I'd thrown a pebble at him in our backyard to see what he would do, and he jumped up and down, making crazy faces and flailing his arms just as he used to.

True, Nachum could say words now. The day before, he'd said an entire sentence.

"The chain. The chain. The chain broked on my bike."

But then the chain was fixed, and he jumped on his bike and was gone, the light in his eyes turned inward, like before.

I asked my mother why Nachum was still crazy. She said I should stop calling him crazy. I asked my mother if he was still retarded. She said I should stop calling him retarded. I asked my mother if the year in Israel had made Nachum cured. "A little bit," she said. "He is better."

My mother said Nachum would go to a special school called Chush. There they would finish curing him. I asked her how long it would take. She smiled at my question.

"Only God knows," she said quietly. "We'll see."

Three

My mother gave Nachum away the summer after first grade. It was then that she told us we were going to Israel to visit family. I had never been to Israel before, had never met my relatives, and my mother said we would have a good time.

In Israel, we had aunts, cousins, and my mother's mother, poised and beautiful as she'd always been. Everyone lived in the holy city of Jerusalem alongside hundreds and thousands of ultraorthodox religious Jews who were just like us. My grandmother lived in the center of the city, in the third-floor apartment of an old stone building, the place where my mother and her two sisters had grown up.

When I told my teacher we were going to Israel, she smiled. She said that I was lucky to be visiting the Holy Land, a place where only Jews lived. Because it was there that the Messiah would take us when he redeemed the Jewish nation from our long exile. And then we'd fly to Jerusalem on the wings of an eagle.

On the plane taking us to the Holy Land, I had pretended that Nachum was not my brother. Instead, I closed my eyes and imagined that I was flying on an eagle. It was hard with my baby brother screeching and Nachum climbing into the overhead compartment. Then he sat down in his seat and began to rock—back, forth, back, forth, as though there was a lullaby deep inside his head, one that only he could hear. The lady across from me stared at him wide-eyed. I nodded sympathetically. He was not my brother. Nachum only stopped rocking once the plane took off.

Ten sticky hours later, we arrived in the Holy Land. We stood around my mother, six children waiting for a dozen suitcases. I wanted to run ahead to the suitcases, tumbling like bowling balls out of the gaping mouth of the baggage tunnel, but my mother did not let me. Instead, she sternly told me and my four-year-old sister, Miri, to stand this close, to each hold one of Nachum's hands, and to never let go. Then she turned, pushing the baggage cart ahead.

I glumly held Nachum's pinky finger as we marched toward the conveyor belt. That's when I saw that there were goyim in Israel. They were all over, in every corner and space. In fact, I barely saw any Jews.

I let go of Nachum's pinky finger. Miri looked at me. Then she let go too.

"Where are the Jews?" I asked. My sister shrugged, her thumb wedged securely in her mouth.

"Where are the Jews?" I repeated.

"Jews?" my mother said, placing my whimpering baby brother in his carriage. "Here. There. Everywhere."

I looked everywhere. I saw men without *kippas,* in jeans, women without head coverings wearing pants. Just plain regular goyim like the ones we already had in New York.

I also saw soldiers. They were walking casually among the goyim, in green uniforms and dark berets. The soldiers wore black boots and armbands with symbols on them. Over their shoulders they slung long black guns.

I could not understand. I was looking for the real Jews, men like my father, with beards, *payos,* and large black *kippas.* Women like my mother, with long skirts and wigs covering their hair.

Yitzy said that the people around us were the secular Jews.

"Secular," I repeated. "What are secular Jews?"

"Jews who live like the goyim. They don't live the right way like us. They do sins."

"It can't be," I said. "Israel is filled with Jews, and Jews wear black *kippas.*"

Yitzy said I was stupid. He was already ten, three years older, and knew better.

"Watch the baby," my mother commanded. "Where's Nachum?"

She looked frantically around.

"Nachum? Nachum? Where is he? Where is he?"

Nachum had been right here. Then he was somewhere else. My mother shook her finger angrily in my face, but I told her that it was not my fault. I had held on to Nachum's pinky finger as tight as I could. It was he who had let go.

My mother found Nachum on the other side of the conveyor belt and pulled him back to where we sat impatiently on the shiny floor. She sat him up on top of the suitcase pile, where Yitzy watched him carefully as we waited for the rest of our baggage to come tumbling out.

I asked my mother if it was true what Yitzy said about secular Jews. Heaving a suitcase onto the cart, she said, "The black suitcases are here. Only the blue ones are missing. Rivky, look out for the luggage with the duct tape!"

So I asked her again. And she said yes, yes, it was true. But it was all right. I didn't have to worry. Because one day Mashiach would come, and the *kippa*-less Jews of Israel would repent.

We stayed in Israel for six weeks. Aunt Zahava, my mother's older sister, had found an apartment for us just a few buildings down from where she lived on the corner of Gershon Street.

My mother and Nachum went away a lot. My siblings and I played with our cousins in Aunt Zahava's house. I also played with Chayala, the neighbor, whose birthday was the same as mine.

Chayala showed me how to play *kugelach*, a children's game of toss and catch using five cubic stones. She also taught me fast Hebrew songs. One day she took me to the tiny corner grocery to buy a bag of milk for her mother. We sang songs all the way there about the beautiful day, about God the Almightiest, and about the Messiah, who'd come tomorrow.

Just then a soldier turned a corner. He passed us with his

long black gun. The soldier did not look at us but strode ahead in his big boots, the gun swinging on his back.

I stared. I asked Chayala if the soldier was a real Jew. Chayala said that he was, but not the right kind. "Good Jews don't fight," she explained. "He is one of the Jews who don't keep the Torah or daven. They believe in strength and killing, not in *Emunah Ba'Hashem*, faith in God. Jews like us do not join the army. We don't wear green uniforms or hold guns. Good Jews pray to Heaven and study the Torah. That is why Israel is always saved."

I wondered if the soldier knew this. I wondered if he knew that he was going to hell. Chayala said a girl in her class had a brother who went mad one day and joined the army. Everyone in the community prayed for his soul but it was too late. In the army, he fell in love. He fell in love with another soldier—a lady kind. The worst kind of all.

The boy's father, Chayala said, did not leave the house for weeks, so great was his humiliation. As for the soldier and the lady, they moved away and nobody ever saw them again.

I sighed sympathetically. Chayala nodded. "This is what happens if you go into the army," she said.

On the last day of our trip in Israel, my mother took me and Rivky to the hills outside Jerusalem where my ancestors were buried.

The hills outside Jerusalem are a holy place. Thousands of Jews lie beneath their sacred ground, and it is here that descendants and followers come to pray, putting pebbles on fading gravestones, asking the departed for help from the heavens.

My mother handed me a laminated sheet and told me to

recite the psalms printed on it, but I didn't want to. It was hot in the hills, and outside the small mausoleum where my ancestors lay buried there was no shade from the vengeful sun. Bored and irritated, I wandered between the uneven lines of graves, gathering pebbles left on headstones into neat little mounds. Then I sat in the mausoleum, watching my mother and sister pray as two bearded men stood outside, patiently waiting for them to finish.

Other men waited behind those two because my ancestors had been holy men, and many came to pray at their graves.

After we left, Rivky said that it was disrespectful to be bored in a graveyard, and forbidden to play with pebbles left for the sacred dead. But I stuck my tongue out at my goody-goody sister and her righteous babble.

"I made the messy pebbles into neat piles," I told her. "The sacred dead like it much better that way."

"No, they don't," Rivky said. "The dead don't care about such things."

"Yes, they do," I said loudly. "They don't want pebbles all messed up on their graves."

Rivky turned to my mother, waiting for her agreement, but my mother said that it really didn't matter.

"We're going to Aunt Itta now. Enough with the fighting."

Aunt Itta and Uncle Zev and their daughters, Ayalah and Batya, also lived in Jerusalem, in a fourth-floor apartment on a road near the bottom of a hill. The street they lived on was called Rabbi Yehuda or Rabbi Shimon Street. Or maybe it was Rabbi Levy Street. In Jerusalem many streets are named after rabbis. I just called it Rabbi Holy Man Street.

Aunt Itta and Uncle Zev did not have air-conditioning. They said they did not need any on Rabbi Holy Man Street. Jerusalem's air was pure and fresh, and when you breathed it in, you no longer felt hot.

This was not true. I had breathed Jerusalem's air all day long, both in and out, and I was still hot.

In the fourth-floor apartment, my sixteen-year-old cousin Ayalah told me to stop whining.

"Come here, and stand by the windows," she said. "See the beautiful hills? Here you feel the breeze." Then she gave me sugar puffs and brushed my hair, twisting it into two short braids.

Fourteen-year-old Batya, the gentler one, smiled and gave me four colorful erasers. "I have more," she said very quietly. "I'll give them to you when your sisters aren't looking."

I liked my cousin Batya, with her bouncing black curls and pleasant, round face. I also liked her because she said that I was very sweet. I liked Ayalah too, just not as much. She was more serious, less cheerful, her dark eyes more reserved. Ayalah was taller and thinner than her sister and did not have the same easy laugh, but Aunt Itta said that Ayalah was very smart. When she finished high school, she would study for a degree in special education. I wasn't sure what that meant, but I knew that to pursue it you had to be very smart.

My uncle Zev, my father's brother and a renowned scholar, sat at the table studying a holy book. He looked up every once in a while and smiled. With his almost white beard and gentle eyes, he looked very nearly like a saint. My aunt, with her plain, chin-length wig and old-fashioned glasses perched on the bridge of her nose, looked just like the matronly wife of a near saint. I had three more cousins, all boys, but one was already married, and the other two were in yeshiva somewhere, where they studied the Torah all day.

Everyone hovered over Nachum. My mother and aunt conversed in low, urgent tones, watching my brother, who sat by himself in the corner, setting colored wooden blocks in perfect patterns and rocking softly back and forth. I chased Miri around the dining room table until we broke a glass cup.

Then we said our good-byes. Back at the apartment we had rented, Aunt Zahava and her husband, Tzvi, helped carry down our suitcases. Then we drove in a white taxi to the airport in Tel Aviv. Nachum did not come with us. He stayed with Aunt Itta and Uncle Zev on Rabbi Holy Man Street in Jerusalem, near the bottom of the hill.

On the plane going back to New York, I watched a Disney movie. As my siblings and mother slept, I ate the bag of meringues that she had hidden in the carry-on, the ones Aunt Itta had made for us for the way home. When my mother woke up and saw what I'd done, she was really angry. I said I was sorry but I was not.

I did not ask my mother why Nachum had stayed, or if he'd ever come back. It was good enough that he was gone.

Back home in Flatbush, my cousin Shaindel asked why Nachum had not come back with us.

I shrugged. "Don't know," I said, slurping my dripping cherry Popsicle.

"Is it 'cause he's cuckoo?" she wanted to know.

I licked my fingers, then stuck out my tongue as far as I could.

"Is my tongue red like blood?" I asked.

Shaindel said it wasn't.

I ignored her question about my brother and went to the bathroom to look in the mirror and see for myself whether my tongue was red like blood.

Things were quiet in our home without Nachum. He was only a year younger than I was, but we had never played together. Nachum played only by himself. When I tried to share with him, he blinked, flailed his hands, and sometimes gave a piercing shriek, and I didn't want to play with him anymore. It was better when he was away. And after our trip to Israel, I thought things would stay like that forever.

Four

My best friend, Blimi, said that it was my parents' fault my brother was crazy, because they had fallen in love.

I chased Blimi down the school hallway when she said this. I stuck out my tongue at her. I told her that she was a liar and had no right to say such things about my family.

"It's true," Blimi said. "I even heard my father talking about it on the phone." She stood across from me, her chin jutting out, her ponytail bouncing up and down. "Everybody knows!" she exclaimed. "Your parents fell in love before they were married! I'm not making up lies!"

I glowered at Blimi. I stuck out my tongue again.

She stuck out hers at me. Then she ran away.

I wasn't friends with her all that week.

That day, after school, Kathy told me not to feel bad about what Blimi had said. There was nothing wrong with falling in love.

Kathy was our neighbor. She lived in the third-floor attic apartment of my house and we were good friends. This was a problem because Kathy was many years older than me—my sister Rivky said she was fifty at least—and married. Also, because she had had a nervous breakdown some years back and had been childish and strange ever since. But more important, Kathy was a goy. And we did not play with goyim.

In the neighborhood of Borough Park, in the borough of Brooklyn, where everyone I knew lived, there were few gentiles. Mostly, there were Jews, ultraorthodox Jews, all of the holy nation picked by God in the Sinai desert three thousand years ago. But in Flatbush, where my family lived, there were mostly goyim, people who were unchosen, like Kathy.

Kathy was a real goy, of the Christian type. She went to church every Sunday. So I should not have been friends with her at all. My sister had told me that it was just plain wrong, prancing around with a goy like that. She said my teacher would never approve. And Mrs. Friedman really did not approve. Kathy might be a sweet lady, she said, but I should find other friends to talk with. It was wrong. God would not allow for it.

God, truly, did not allow for it. He said so Himself, clearly, somewhere in the Torah: that His people should not play with the goyim, even if they are the neighbors. Because Kathy had not been in the desert two thousand years before. She did not keep Shabbos or kosher. She did not know how to pray to God in Hebrew. She did not observe the rules of modesty. She wore pants.

But I liked Kathy anyway. I went to her often after school and she gave me kosher candies. I told her all about the new art notebook I had gotten, and she showed me pictures of herself when she was a girl.

I asked Kathy several times not to go to church. I explained that if she'd only be gentile without being quite so gentile, God wouldn't mind so much that I was her friend. But she just laughed.

Kathy had a very good memory. She remembered when I was born, eight years earlier, on the fifteenth of August.

"You were a beautiful baby," she said. "Always giggling and laughing, with eyes like pretty green stars."

She said the same about my little sister, Miri, and my brother Avrumi, but she almost never spoke about Nachum, although she remembered the day he was born, before anyone knew he was crazy. As a baby, Nachum hadn't giggled and laughed. He had screamed for hours on end, even when my mother held him, even when she cradled him on the soft grass in the garden outside.

The day Blimi said that awful thing about love, I ran upstairs to Kathy's. She smiled a little. Then she said, "It's nice, falling in love."

I didn't answer. It was hard for her to understand, I knew. Goyim fall in love and back out of it all the time. But Chassidish Jews, we know better. Marriage is a sacred business, decided by God, and the bride and groom have nothing to do with it.

Kathy told me about when she was twenty-two and became engaged to her husband, Mark. "He brought me flowers, and took me on trips, and we had a wedding in a garden." She looked happy, remembering.

Kathy loved speaking of Mark and how she had married him—and was still married to him after over thirty years—but I didn't like Mark very much. He was silent and gruff, a scary kind of goy, barely answering me when I passed him by as he smoked cigarettes right outside our house.

I sang Kathy a song I had learned in school, but I couldn't remember the motions that went with it. Then I hurried back down to the first floor, before anyone could ask where I'd been.

After supper, I told Rivky what Blimi had said.

"That Blimi is a blabbermouth," Rivky said. "She's slandering others, which is an evil sin. Don't be friends with her anymore."

"I know," I said. "I know. I'm not being best friends with her this whole week."

My brother was crazy for other reasons. God did not make crazy like that for nothing. It was all part of His Grand Master Plan, the one Mrs. Friedman always said explained the tragedies and mysteries of the earth, and showed that everything was all for the best. The problem with God's Grand Master Plan was that it was a hidden one, an eternal secret known only to saints, angels, and souls on high. This meant that I had to die if I wanted to find out why Nachum was really crazy, and I wasn't going to die anytime soon.

Upon realizing this, I had asked my mother if I could get to Heaven sooner, say by noon tomorrow, so I wouldn't have to wait so many more years just to understand one heavenly secret.

My mother just looked at me. "Do your homework," she said.

Over the years, I had heard other reasons why Nachum was plain crazy. My cousin Shaindel told me that her cousin's aunt from her father's side told her that it was because my mother didn't nurse Nachum when he was a baby. If only she had nursed him, God would've changed his Grand Master Plan, and Nachum would have never turned out this way. Mrs. Olephsky, from the summer colony, said the nurse in the hospital must have dropped him on his head but was scared to tell anyone, leaving him damaged and forcing God to immediately make a new plan: make Nachum crazy. My ten-year-old neighbor, Motti, said that if we would only repent, my brother would become uncrazy. God would remember his original plan and see to it that Nachum was as whole as anyone, and it did not matter who had dropped him on his head.

I knew that what they said probably wasn't true, though I was never completely certain. But then Rebbitzen Goldknup, the *rav*'s wife and my mother's good friend, told me the story of the angel who struck Nachum's lip just a tad too hard before he was ever born.

It is true, it says so in the Talmud, that before a child is born, an angel from on high studies with him the words and secrets of the Torah, so that his soul is suffused with holiness. Then, at the moment before birth, the angel reaches out with his right hand and strikes the upper lip of the unborn child, erasing all memory from its mind. This way, the child must start again. This way, he must put in his own effort to regain the lost knowledge.

But sometimes the angel strikes the upper lip too hard. In this case, not only is the memory of the Torah erased, but so is the ability of the child to remember anything, even how to speak, how to say simple words. Such a child is born mad, like my brother.

When I told this to my brother Yitzy, he frowned. "Not true," he said. "Everyone makes up stories." He knew exactly when it had happened, though he could not really say how it was part of any grand plan. It was, he explained to me, because of the boiling milk that had spilled on Nachum's brain when he was only two. My mother had put a pot of milk on the stove to cook, and then, just as it was bubbling, Nachum had reached up and grabbed the handle. The pan toppled over. The boiling milk spilled right over my brother's head, and for weeks he was wrapped in bandages like a mummy. When they took the bandages off, Nachum was broken.

I thought this was a good reason, so a few days later, when I was playing at Blimi's house, I explained it all to her. But Blimi rolled her eyes.

"It's the love thing," she said again, "and anyway, there's no such thing as turning crazy from milk."

I chased Blimi angrily across the yard. I pulled her hair. I called her a liar and other things, until she ran up the stairs and inside, locking the door of her house.

I sat in Blimi's yard and crossed my arms. Just because Blimi was two months older than me, she thought she knew better. She did not.

Later, I told Kathy that Blimi was a hateful liar. She was just jealous because I had a bigger collection of Hello Kitty stickers, and because my family was much more important than hers.

Five

I asked my father if it was true that he had fallen in love with my mother. My father, pouring milk into his coffee, burst out laughing.

I scowled.

He leaned against the dairy counter, laughing harder. The coffee sloshed over the rim of his cup, dripping onto the beige tiles of the kitchen floor. A small stain grew on the sleeve of his white shirt.

I hid my face behind the cereal box. My mother walked in, a pile of newspapers in the crook of her arm, sheets of paper covered with her writing in her hands.

My father turned to her. "Menuchah wants to know if it's true that we fell in love," he said, and my mother smiled, amused. She put down her papers, sat down across from me at the kitchen table, and chuckled. "What's so funny?" I asked.

"Nothing," my mother said. "Nothing is funny." But I could see the smile hidden in her eyes. She reassured me that they had not fallen in love. They had gotten married because Hashem had wanted them to. Then she turned to her papers and began marking her students' work.

Aha. I knew it. Pious mothers and fathers like mine did not love before, or after, marriage. They did not kiss, or hug, or touch each other in any way. Such things were repulsive to God, and forbidden in a Jewish home. Only liking was allowed—a modest kind of love.

Liking was when my father brought my mother flowers on Tuesday for no reason at all. Liking was when he smacked his lips, declaring her fried eggplant the best he'd ever tasted, even when it was certainly not. Liking was when my father bought my mother a gold necklace when she already had three, when he stuck up for her even when it was plain that I was the one who was right. Liking was when my mother said that my father was the most honest, hardworking man in the world, and she said it proudly, as if it was something special.

Once, my father called my mother a brilliant and "bee-yoo-tiful lady," which was okay, I thought, but somewhat tricky, right where like becomes almost love, and better to stay away from. Besides, mothers aren't "bee-yoo-tiful" ladies. They are mothers. With kerchiefs; long, dark house robes; and purposeful frowns.

So my mother and father liked each other just the way God allowed them to, not more and not less. I asked my father several times more, just to make sure, and he said each time that they had not fallen in love. They had gotten married because Hashem had wanted them to.

I wished Blimi was there right then so I could tell her what my parents had said and yank her ponytail until she begged for mercy. But Blimi was at home in Borough Park, where I was never going to play with her again. And anyway, telling her wouldn't have done much. Because that evening in my father's car, everything got ruined. It was there that Nachum broke the perfect liking between my mother and father.

I can't say how it happened or why, because that's how it was with a brother like Nachum. One minute he was quiet, the next he was blinking mad, as if he'd been struck by the tapping angel once to take away his knowledge of the Torah, once to take away his speech, and once for the rest of his mind.

It began when my father picked my brother and me up from my aunt's apartment, where we had played with my cousins all afternoon. We were riding in my father's new blue minivan, the one with doors that opened automatically. Usually Nachum was quiet in the car. He'd sit peacefully, looking at the dashboard and listening for the spurt and hum of the motor, the throb and pulse of the moving tires, the soft rumble of the road beneath. It was as though the car was his cradle, the engine his lullaby.

But then the sirens came.

My father had stopped at the red light at Seventeenth Avenue and Forty-Seventh Street. From behind us, I could see the ambulance approaching, speeding down the street. My father pulled over to the side of the road to let the ambulance by, siren blaring, and blue and red lights flashed past the windows on Nachum's side. I wanted to tell my father to chase the ambulance down the street, to follow the flashing lights, but just then my brother made a sound like a cat on fire, as if someone had ripped the skin off his chest.

"What happened?" my father shouted, but Nachum didn't answer. He blinked his eyes, his head shooting up like a windup toy's. He threw himself onto the floor in the space between the front and back seats and folded up his body. Then, silently, he began to bang his head forward and back against my father's seat.

Back. Forth.

Back. Forth.

Back. Forth.

Back—

"Stop," my father said. *"Stop that."* His voice was harsh and dark. He could not bear it when Nachum banged his head.

But Nachum could not stop that. Not at home against the wall, not in school against the board, and not in the new blue minivan with the doors that opened automatically.

He banged harder. Back, forth, back, forth, like a swinging ax on wood.

The car behind us beeped loudly. My father, twisted toward Nachum, quickly turned to face front and pressed the gas. Our minivan swerved around the car in front of us and sped down the street toward Flatbush.

Back, forth.

Back, forth.

Back, forth.

Back...

My father's face was pale and grim. He drove quickly down the long block home. We came to an abrupt stop in our driveway. My father jumped out and opened the door on my side.

"Run inside," he said sharply. "Go call Mommy. Fast."

My mother was sitting and writing in the kitchen when I rushed in. I pointed to the backyard.

"Nachum," I exclaimed. "He—" My mother did not wait. She dropped her pen and hurried past me and out the door.

I pulled off my jacket and dragged it down the hall to the bathroom. In the bathroom, I stood on the ledge of the tub and peered through the narrow window overlooking the yard.

It was nearly dark outside, but I could see my father standing away from the van, his legs firmly apart, his hands deep inside his coat pockets. My mother had opened the car door and was leaning in, calling my brother out.

My father was saying something to my mother. I could hear his rising voice, her soft murmuring, as she hovered half in, half out of the car over Nachum. Finally, my mother stood up and looked back at my father, shaking her head, gesturing for him to come.

My father stepped forward. He bent over and into the van. There was a short shriek, a guttural sound, and then my father was standing, carrying my brother in his arms.

But Nachum hated being touched. I could see him, scared and wild, eyes shut tightly, as he hurled himself from my father and crashed onto the asphalt. On his hands and knees, Nachum spun around like a trapped animal trying to escape from between two hunters. My mother reached out to Nachum and circled him closely. She brought her hands down gently over his head, covering his ears, as if trying to shield him from his own terrifying sounds.

Nachum pulled away. He crawled frantically from my mother, bumping into my father's knees. My father stepped back, then forward, gesturing impatiently at my mother as she leaned over Nachum. My brother was standing up now, his hands groping at the space around her, and under the night sky, their shadows looked like two great sea creatures writhing and battling.

Then Nachum turned and ran. He ran down the driveway and out the gate. My mother ran after him. She caught him by the gate, holding him as he struggled, his head nearly crashing into the ground. I could see my mother's shadow pulling back, but my brother's shadow was stronger. It pulled on my mother until it had devoured her, until you could not see what was him and what was her, until it swallowed her whole.

I could hear voices through the narrow window, my mother crying because my father would not come, my father angry because she would not let go, and Nachum screaming and pulling, pulling, pulling.

Six

Sometimes, to give my mother a break, we went to Aunt Tziporah's in Borough Park. Aunt Tziporah was my father's younger sister, and she was the only one besides my mother who knew how to care for Nachum.

Nachum liked going to my aunt's. He liked the soft rug on the bedroom floor in the space between the beds where the toy box stood. There he always played quietly by himself for hours.

My cousins never bothered Nachum. When he walked through the apartment, they quickly made way for him. When he pointed or grabbed, they gave him what he wanted. Aunt Tziporah told my cousins that there was nothing to be afraid of, that Nachum was a special boy, if a little different, and that one day he'd grow out of it and become a great tzaddik, a saint, but they were still scared of him.

Because Nachum was never going to be any saint. No saint would have been struck three times instead of once by the tapping angel. No saint bumped his head against walls and doors. No saint grabbed food from other people's plates. A saint looked deep into the eyes and souls of others. Nachum could not even look at me.

Once, I walked into Nachum's space between the beds in that apartment, looking for a book. My brother, building a tower out of Lego, arched his back and froze, his eyes boring into the door behind me, like a rabbit sensing danger. Saints don't do such things. And I knew all about being a saint. My own family was chock-full of them: rabbis, leaders, and holy men.

Aunt Tziporah told us all about it. She said that my mother came from a noble family, from generations of brilliant rebbes. I loved it when Aunt Tziporah told us stories about my mother and father, and when she spoke of the days when they were young in holy Jerusalem.

Aunt Tziporah knew all about my mother and her royal ancestry. They'd grown up together in Israel, strolling down the narrow lanes and streets of the ancient city. They had been best friends since they met at age fourteen. My aunt always said that my mother was the prettiest girl in Jerusalem. Everyone knew her and her two older sisters, descendants of a noble dynasty, the great rabbinical family of the rebbes of Viyan.

You see, once, before the Holocaust, the Chassidic sect of Viyan had been one hundred thousand strong. There, in the shtetels and towns of eastern Europe, pious Chassidim lived and prayed, paying homage to the Grand Rebbe, my mother's great-grandfather, who resided in the small town of Viyan.

The Grand Rebbe of Viyan was known far and wide as the Vunder Rebbe (the Wonder Rabbi), the man who could make miracles. It was said that even goyim came to him from surrounding villages for advice, a blessing, or a touch of the hand, and that his face shone like that of an angel.

But then came the Holocaust, and Chassidim everywhere were killed. The Grand Rebbe of Viyan was high on the Gestapo's list. They wanted him dead, so the Gestapo sent soldiers and spies deep into the Jewish quarter of Warsaw, promising money and precious sugar for the man who brought in the Vunder Rebbe's head.

But when the Nazi soldiers burst into his building, they could not find him. An SS officer stepped into the rebbe's room, but he saw nothing but a bright light emanating from the corner. The officer squinted, shielding his face. When he walked out, he declared to the others that the room was empty.

"When the Germans set their eyes on him," Aunt Tziporah told me, "they saw only the sun."

In 1941, as the Nazis turned the ghetto upside down, the Vunder Rebbe miraculously escaped. With the help of well-bribed officers, he and a few family members made their way to Jerusalem on the last boat out of Europe.

In Jerusalem, the Vunder Rebbe sat in his small room, waiting. He waited for his disciples to return to him from the ashes and horrors of Europe. But there were few survivors, and when they stumbled onto the shores of Israel in 1945, they found their rebbe a frail and sickly man. He gathered them close around him, but all the loss was too much. His broken heart left the earth in 1948, and his eldest son, my mother's great-uncle, a fierce and saintly leader, became the next rebbe of Viyan.

My Aunt Tziporah remembered this fierce and saintly leader from when she was a young girl in Jerusalem. She had seen him, with his long white beard and dark, fiery eyes, striding down the main street toward the shul, crowds of disciples rushing behind him.

"Even the air trembled around him," she said.

The new rebbe told his Chassidim that they would rebuild. There would be new life, a future of thriving towns and cities brimming with the sounds of song, just like the world his father, the Vunder Rebbe, had left behind. Once more, their people would hold their heads high.

I leaned on the table in my Aunt Tziporah's small kitchen and rested my chin in the palm of my hand, watching her peel tangerines. Aunt Tziporah spoke cheerfully as she stood over an open trash can, her dark hair peeking out from beneath her kerchief.

Both my aunt and my mother had grown up in Jerusalem, but they had lived in different parts of the city. This was why they did not know each other until the first day of ninth grade in the central religious girls' high school. I had heard the story from my aunt many times, but every time she told it as if it were brand-new.

It was the first week in September, and two days after classes had begun. The teacher had finished roll call and was pacing in front of her desk, about to begin. Suddenly, the door swung open. Into the room walked a girl, tall, slender, and confident. She strode across the classroom as though the wind had blown her in, her long red hair cascading over her shoulders.

The teacher's eyes narrowed. She tapped her fingers on the desk. She waited for an explanation, an apology, a late note, perhaps. But the redheaded girl said nothing. She sat at an empty desk, flipped back her hair, and then took out a notebook and began to write in long, graceful lettering.

The teacher cleared her throat.

The girl with the red hair looked up.

"My name's Esther Strauss," she said calmly. "There was a family wedding."

The teacher's mouth opened, then closed. Descendants of noble rebbes did not need late notes.

My aunt chuckled. "It was good being her friend. You could get away with anything."

I switched my chin from my right palm to my left and frowned. I, too, was a descendant of noble rebbes, by only one generation more, yet in my school I always needed a late note. The only time my teacher said anything about my holy ancestors was when I did not behave.

"What would your great-grandmother Rebbitzen Miril say?" Mrs. Friedman had asked me after I poked Chaya Sarah's back in the middle of class. "Such *hieligeh* grandparents and this is how you behave?"

I had badly wanted to tell Mrs. Friedman that I poked Chaya Sarah's back with the sharp point of my pencil not because of my holy ancestors, but because Chaya Sarah was annoying. But she did not allow me to explain.

Aunt Tziporah told us more such stories around the kitchen table, and I listened, entranced. Then, after supper, my father came and said it was time to head home.

Yitzy, Rivky, Miri, and I raced down the stairs to my father's van, shouting about whose turn it was to press the button for the automatic doors. Nachum came after us, a picture book Aunt Tziporah had given him in his hand. Then my father drove us to our home in faraway Flatbush, under the railroad bridge and to the other side, where the goyim lived.

Seven

There were only ten girls in the little yellow van that took my sisters and me home from school. Everyone else at our all-girls school in Borough Park crowded onto the large buses that dropped them off within the same neighborhood, where all proper Chassidic Jews lived. But every day at four o'clock, the little yellow van drove in the opposite direction, past the tracks, past where the trains ran, all the way to the gentile-filled neighborhood of Flatbush.

My family lived three blocks deep into the goyim, among Italians and Syrians and many others—Jews too, but the kind who watched TV and whose women wore pants. It was here that my father had bought a great white house with a large yard and a red fence. He bought it when my mother was still pregnant with me, so I never had a chance to tell him my opinion: that there was no sense in buying a house on Avenue I when we could have settled on Seventeenth Avenue, right by the shul and my school.

Only two Chassidic families lived near us on Avenue I: the Fines and the Cohens, two blocks down. On Halloween, Christmas, and all the *goyishe* holidays, my sisters and I, the Fines, and the Cohen twins were taken home early in the yellow van because it was dangerous for Jews to be out at dusk. Drunken goyim might throw eggs at us or do other evil things.

Ruchela and Leah Cohen, the twins, were a year younger than me but we were good friends. We had our own secret spy gang and played robbers and pirates and had all sorts of fun. We built a tree house from cardboard, staged puppet shows in the basement, and even dug a deep bunker in our yard to hide from Nazis, but they never showed up.

In the summers, the Cohens went to the same summer colony as my family, up in the Catskill Mountains, and we had adventures there too. Once, Ruchela said we were so close we must be secret first cousins, but I said that couldn't be true because they wore denim skirts. My mother would never let me wear a denim skirt. Denim was a modern, immodest material, unbecoming of a Jewish girl.

Blimi, though she did not live anywhere near me, was my true best friend. She did not wear denim either. But Blimi almost never came to my house in Flatbush because her mother thought it was too far and dangerous, and because Blimi was scared of the goyim.

The first time Blimi came to play with me was on a Friday, two weeks after Nachum came home. She had agreed only because her mother was in the hospital after having her ninth baby, and Blimi was staying with her aunt, who had errands to run before Shabbos.

I reassured Blimi that we were safe, that the gentiles never started trouble with me because I was a Yid. Anyway, God would come to my rescue in one second. So Blimi had sat in the first seat in the yellow van with me. She stared, wide-eyed, out the window. She said she had never been out of Borough Park before, and already it looked so different.

I shrugged knowingly.

"That's not Flatbush yet," I explained. "It's Webster Avenue, right near Flatbush."

Blimi pressed her nose against the window.

"You're not scared to live there?" she asked.

I munched casually on a potato chip.

"Only sometimes," I said. "Like when my neighbors started a fire and danced around it at night and they were dressed like the Ku Klux Klan." I took another chip. "Then my father said a special prayer and they disappeared. Poof. Like that."

Blimi looked at me, shocked. I nodded for emphasis.

Blimi said Borough Park was bigger than Flatbush because Borough Park was where all the real *frum* Jews lived.

I told Blimi that it was not so.

"Borough Park is better," I agreed. "But Flatbush is for sure bigger."

"Uh-uh," Blimi said as though I was mad. "Everyone knows. Flatbush is much smaller."

"It is not."

"It is too."

"Is not." I licked the salt off my finger. "I even saw it on a map once."

Blimi scrunched up her nose. "So something is wrong with your map. Everyone knows."

The van came to a halt. The doors squealed open. The driver shouted at us to stop chattering and get off. He didn't have all day. Go, go, *go!*

I ran up the front steps of my house, Blimi skipping gaily behind me. I threw open the door, shouted hello, and pushed Blimi quickly into my room. I did not want her to see Nachum. I had asked my mother that morning to hide my brother when Blimi came, but she had refused.

"Try playing with him instead," my mother had said. "Be nice for once, instead of shoving him and fighting!"

But I couldn't do that. It was dangerous to play with Nachum. He might kick me, or blink creepily at me. Besides, he was a boy. It wasn't modest.

For us, the true religious, boys and girls didn't play together. From the age of three, girls and boys went to separate schools, separate pools, and prayed in separate parts of the shul, the girls with their mothers behind the partition, the boys with their fathers in front. It had always been this way among the pious, because terrible things happened when girls and boys mingled, even among family—Blimi's older cousin, Nechy, had told her so.

Nechy was nine years old when her eleven-year-old cousin Z'vulin suddenly stopped playing with her. This happened after Z'vulin's rebbe told him that it was a terrible sin to play with a girl, even if she was your cousin. And if they played, the rebbe warned, especially when nobody saw, God would make a baby come. The only girls a boy could play with after the age of three were his own sisters.

Nechy had told Z'vulin that he didn't know what he was talking about—cousins could still play; she was almost like his sister—but Z'vulin said his rebbe surely knew better than her and he refused to be alone in the same room with her ever again. He did not want a baby to come.

I didn't know if a baby would come or how, but I decided to be extra modest, just in case. Maybe God didn't mind if I played with my brother, but I wasn't going to chance it, not with such a boy. Soon, though, Blimi got bored locked up in my room. She said she really wanted to go out; it was stupid just talking on the bed. So I let Blimi look at my Hello Kitty stickers and showed her how to turn a cartwheel. Then we drew funny faces on the back of my underpants and jumped up and down on my bed.

That's when I saw Mark coming up the steps outside the window of my room. I pulled Blimi down quickly, whispering that we hadn't shut the shades and it was a sin if Mark saw.

"Mark?" Blimi said. "Who's Mark?"

Kathy's husband, I told her. The goyim who lived upstairs.

Blimi said it was crazy that I had actual gentiles living upstairs, but I told her it was okay. The Almighty protected us from evil at all times.

She begged me to take her upstairs so she could see the goyim, but I told her that it was dangerous because Mark, unlike Kathy, was dark and silent, and he smoked fat brown cigarettes with gold stickers on them, sometimes right by our door.

Blimi looked at me, her mouth open. She said she really wanted to go home now.

I changed my mind. I told her that I was joking. If Mark ever smoked a fat brown cigarette outside our door, my father would kick him out of the house that very day. Anyway, I reassured her, my father said sixteen special psalms every night, and sixteen special psalms every dawn, and those special psalms protected us from any curse or evil that a gentile might try.

My father never forgot those psalms, I explained. He said them fervently twice a day—except for once. It happened some years back when my father was ill, and at dawn he slept late, forgetting the prayers. Eventually he got up and remembered, but only at noon, and for several hours there had been no heavenly protection. Though my father then quickly said the psalms, it was too late. Nachum had already been cursed. The goyim's evil had struck him, penetrating his very soul. And that's why my brother was crazy.

Blimi listened quietly. She thought about it for a while, and then decided that it made sense. She said she felt terrible about blaming my parents all along. Nachum wasn't crazy because they fell in love. It was the black magic that did it, the gentiles' terrible curse. Goyim did such things, especially to children of such noble ancestry.

I nodded, relieved. Why hadn't I thought of this before?

"I knew it was Mark's fault the entire time," I told Blimi. "I just didn't want to say it out loud."

Blimi's aunt came by shortly afterward to pick her up. I opened the door to my room and Blimi ran out, tripping right over Nachum's big head where he had settled it on the floor outside my bedroom.

Nachum was looking at a box of colorful blocks, his eyes never moving off the picture on the front of the box.

Blimi stood up, staring.

I pushed her toward the front door. I told her that it was really late and she had to leave, but she kept looking back at Nachum.

I told Blimi that dinner wasn't ready yet and I had to help my mother in the kitchen, but she pulled on her coat as slowly as possible, still watching my crazy brother.

I said, "Okay, good-bye! Good-bye!," blocking her way so she couldn't see. But she looked over my shoulder until her aunt took her hand, and I closed the door in her face.

I thought of kicking Nachum's box of blocks. Instead, I went into my room, climbed into my blanket box, and thought about the annoying mysteries of God.

Eight

When my mother was a child, she posed for many pictures all dressed up and elegant in frilly clothes. It was my grandmother who took the pictures, or the man at the studio under the black cloth, flashing the smoking bulb.

There were many photographs of my mother and her sisters in sterile white rooms, in wedding halls, and under the bright Jerusalem sun. Others showed cousins and close friends smiling prettily into the camera, the white stones of the city sparkling behind them. But there was one photo that was my favorite, and I hid it under the socks in my drawer so I could look at it often.

The picture, faded and worn, showed my grandfather sitting in a chair, his eyes crinkled, his *shtreimel*—the round fur hat worn by Chassidim on the Sabbath, holidays, and special family occasions—sitting crooked on his head. My mother is standing next to him in a white dress, dainty pink flowers in her hair. She is thirteen years old. Her arm is wrapped around

her father's neck and she is laughing. My grandfather is looking lovingly at her, smiling gently through his soft gray beard.

"They were the aristocrats," Aunt Tziporah said, as I
squeezed a strawberry through the gap in my teeth, the juice
squirting right into Yitzy's eye. He glared at me.

"They lived where the rich did," my aunt continued. "Right
in the center of the city, far from the border and the poor side
of town."

Everyone in Jerusalem knew the three Strauss sisters:
Chana, Zahava, and Esther, great-nieces of the Grand Rebbe
of Viyan. They were the daughters of Reb Menachem Baruch
Strauss, the newspaper publisher, and granddaughters of Reb
Naphtali Strauss, the Knesset minister, and Bubba Miril, the
only sister of the Holy Rebbe and a woman so wise the rebbe
himself consulted with her nearly every day.

My great-grandfather, the Knesset minister, had a government car. In the grand synagogue on Geulah Street, he stood,
along with my grandfather, in the front row, right next to
his brother-in-law, the Holy Rebbe. In the women's section
on the second floor, up front, there was a chair that only
my grandmother could sit in and pray in, right next to her
mother-in-law, Bubba Miril, and the rebbe's own modest wife.

"She was the queen of the neighborhood, that grandmother of yours," Aunt Tziporah said, shaking her head. "The
beautiful Miriam Strauss, with porcelain skin and designer
clothes, survivor of one of the oldest Chassidic families of
Viyan."

My aunt plucked a strawberry from the bowl.

"When she clicked down the street in those four-inch heels,

I'm telling you, men's blood pressures tripled. She wore the most expensive clothing and jewelry. She must have had twenty pairs of shoes—one for each outfit."

My beautiful grandmother, Miriam, was a devout and religious woman, pious and also vain. This meant that she shopped almost as much as she prayed, and that she observed the rules of fashion every bit as strictly as she observed the Ten Commandments. It is perfectly acceptable to be both pious and vain. Many women live this way, and God doesn't mind at all.

My Savtah Miriam also baked cakes for the Holy Rebbe, the only ones he would eat. But mainly she shopped—"On Dizengoff," my aunt explained. "Dizengoff, Tel Aviv, the Fifth Avenue of the land"—because she loved beautiful things, and after what she'd been through with the Holocaust and all, nobody could judge her.

When my grandmother first arrived in Israel after the war, at the age of sixteen, she was the only surviving member of her family. But one day the news came. A Chassid ran frantically down the street, pounding on the door of her home.

"Your brother Mordcha' is alive!" the Chassid shouted. "Your brother Mordcha' is alive!"

Not only was her older brother alive, but he was here, in Jerusalem, having just arrived at the port of Haifa a few days before from the ravages of Europe.

Savtah Miriam and her close friend Yehudis hurried to the central bus station where Mordcha' waited. But when she saw from afar the brother she had not seen in over two years, she stopped. She turned away.

"What happened?" Yehudis asked. "Your brother is waiting!"

But Miriam would not take another step. Her back to Mordcha', she told Yehudis that she would not greet her brother when he looked like a goy. Why was his head bare? Is this what their murdered father and ancestors saw when they looked down from Heaven? A son without a *kippa*, without a hat, discarding their past as if it were a disposable thing? Until he put on a hat, she would not recognize him.

So Yehudis went to tell Mordcha' that his sister would not see him, not until his head was covered in respect for God. My grandmother's only surviving brother ran hastily through the crowd until he found a Chassid who lent him his hat. He then returned to his sister, dressed as a Jew, and she smiled and wept and embraced him.

Though my devout grandmother loved shopping, my mother did not. She read books, wrote poetry, and spent time with her father at the newspaper instead.

"Your intelligent mother had no patience for fashion," Aunt Tziporah said. "She owned a few tops, a few skirts, and that was it. She was interested in history and literature. She and your grandfather, they were this close." She held up two fingers, twisting one around the other.

I had always known that my mother had been dearly close with her father. She spoke often of him, of his generosity and wisdom. She had named my brother Nachum after him, as he was the first son born to her after her father's unexpected death. My grandfather, the publisher, had written more than thirty-five books, and they lined the shelves of my mother's study. He wrote books about the world before it was turned upside down by the Nazis, when the Jews of Europe were still alive, and the Chassidim of Viyan still strong. He wrote about a lost world of synagogues and mikvahs, about centuries-old communities whose only remains now lay in the bottomless pits of ash of Auschwitz.

When my mother was a young child, my grandfather traveled to America for months at a time doing research and writing the stories of the dead. While he was gone, my mother slept in his bed. She wrapped herself in her father's nightshirt, calling to him in her sleep, hiding the shirt each morning in her drawer so that her mother could not find it and wash out the warmth and smell of her father, who was across the sea.

Sometimes I saw my mother cry for him as if he had just died. Sometimes she looked at my grandfather's portrait on the mantel above the fireplace in our dining room and tears streamed down her face. Once, on Shabbos, before Nachum returned from Israel, my mother had burst into tears while speaking of her father, ten years after he'd passed away.

"My little Esther'la," he had called her. "My redheaded beauty, youngest and smartest of them all."

Nine

It was fall in Borough Park—and also in Flatbush—and I watched the leaves dropping to the ground from the tall elm trees leaning over our garden. They fell slowly, waltzing and twirling through the air, until the breeze settled them gently on the sidewalk right by our red fence.

I loved jumping on fall leaves, and one day, after the little yellow school van had driven away, I ran to the corner of our yard. There the leaves spun into colorful mounds. Rivky, ignoring me, went up the steps and into the house.

I danced under the elm tree. I hopped and jumped on the dried-out leaves, listening to the crackle they made only in the fall. My sister had asked me to save some leaves for her, not to use up all the rustling and crunch, but I had not saved her even one.

Twenty minutes had passed. Maybe a half hour. I had stomped the life out of every last leaf. I looked up at the tree, my face in the wind, and then chased the ones just falling, clapping the bits of red, yellow, and orange between my hands before they ever touched the ground. But from the window of the study at the back of the house there came a hard knocking. I looked up. My mother motioned angrily from behind the glass, her eyes blazing. I'd better get inside right now.

I went inside immediately, but she was still furious. "You worried the very soul out of my body!" she shouted. "Where in heaven's name have you been? What exactly have you been waiting for? For me to call the police?"

I pointed at Rivky. "She knew where I was!"

But Rivky just shrugged. "No, I didn't," she said. "You just disappeared."

She studied my flushed pink face.

"You look like a fat tomato," she added.

I followed my mother down the hall to the room in the back of the house. On the way there I tried explaining, but she informed me that I was simply and incorrigibly irresponsible, thoughtless, and would one day give her a heart attack. Then she handed me a garbage bag and told me to stand there.

"And don't move," she ordered. "I'm cleaning the closet before it caves in from the weight of its own mess."

The room in the back of the house belonged to my mother. My father had built it when they first bought the house as a place for my mother to work, because besides being a teacher, my mother was a researcher and a writer. The shelves of her study were lined with hundreds of books: books on history, books on the Holocaust, books by my grandfather and others. The shelves reached up to the ceiling.

Against the opposite wall and across from the books stood

metal filing cabinets with drawers that would not open, no matter how much I pulled. And near the cabinets was a spacious closet with large, deep shelves filled from top to bottom with teachers' notebooks, rolls of fax paper, and other supplies.

My friend's mother once said that my mother had a brilliant mind, just like her father and grandfathers, and that if she had been a man, she could have been a rebbe.

Every few months, my mother, in her long navy house robe, her red hair tucked hastily under a kerchief, would declare, "I have no idea what's going on in my own closet. If the Messiah himself shows up, I'm not budging—not till this mess is cleared up."

Rivky usually helped my mother organize the shelves and clear out the rubbish, and my mother would call her "my little *tzaddekes,* my own little saint."

I did not mind that my mother called Rivky a little *tzaddekes* because I did not care to be a saint, big or little, and would rather read a book in my room. But now I was forced to help with the mess because my mother was really, truly mad at me. Glaring down from the chair she stood on, she said that if I knew what was good for me, I had better put my two hands to use without so much as a pout or a whine.

I held open the garbage bag, all the way up to my chin, as my mother tossed in crumpled papers from the top shelf. Eventually, she forgot how mad she was and her face relaxed. Then she began telling me stories about my great-grandmother, the wise Bubba Miril, whom she had dearly loved, and my great-grandfather, the one who had been Knesset minister and whose penetrating gaze followed us from his portrait, which hung on our dining room wall.

My great-grandfather, Reb Naphtali, had been an important man in Jerusalem, a member of Ben-Gurion's cabinet for eight years. On Shabbos night, after prayers at the synagogue, the Chassidim pressed his hand in respect before moving to the Grand Rebbe to wish him *ah guten Shabbos*. On weekdays, they made way for him in the streets.

Reb Naphtali had signed his name on Israel's declaration of independence, but only after Ben-Gurion had agreed that Israel would be a Jewish state. He had joined the government coalition in 1948 as minister of welfare, but only after the future prime minister promised that Shabbos would be the official day of rest, and that young scholars studying the holy Torah would not be drafted into the army.

As my mother talked, she worked her way to the lower shelves, eventually pushing away the chair she'd been standing on. Then, unexpectedly, she knelt on the floor in front of the closet. It was then, right in the middle of the story, that she slid her hands into a narrow opening by the threshold and, with one quick motion, pulled up the closet floor.

I gasped.

There beneath the trapdoor was a secret drawer, a deep and mysterious space. There under the closet lay albums, documents, and gifts wrapped in shimmering paper, buried like hidden treasure.

My mother pulled out a box. She opened it, then closed it, and put it back in its place. She moved things in and out of the drawer, this way and that, and after a few minutes slapped her hands, wiping off the dust. Then, gripping the slab of linoleum-covered floor, she firmly pushed it back down.

I stared in amazement. Then I asked my mother if I could open the floor myself.

"No way," she said.

I asked her if I could open it on my birthday, just once, but she looked at me sternly and said the same thing.

"Do not touch the closet," she said. "Do you hear me? There are no toys in there." Then she handed me a teacher's gray roll book, a prize for my good behavior, and walked out, the garbage bag dragging behind her.

I stood in the middle of the room and stared at the closet door. Just a few seconds ago, it had been plain and brown. There were stains at the bottom, scratches on the sides, and the doorknob didn't turn all the way. But now the broken doorknob was forbidden. Now, beneath the trapdoor, there were secrets.

I dropped the teacher's roll book on the floor. I didn't want it. I no longer cared for prizes or stories. I just wanted to pull up the secret floor and search the mysteries beneath.

That evening I asked my father if he could please let me do exactly as I wanted, and not ask any questions at all. To my great surprise, he said no.

Usually he said yes. When I wanted something, I'd simply ask my father and he'd say, "Of course. For my best duh'ter—anyt'ing!" Then my mother would come in and ruin it. Like the time my father gave me a whole container of ice cream at midnight when I couldn't fall asleep, but my mother made me put most of it back. And like the time I wanted an entire bar of white chocolate, and my father gave me two, but then Rivky saw and told my mother, who said that half a bar was bad enough and forced me to share. And like all the other times.

My mother was the decider, the grand sayer of yes and no in our home. My father's job was to agree. So that evening, while my mother was out, I ran to my father breathlessly. I grabbed his hand just as soon as he walked in the door and dragged him down the hall to the last room.

"Abba, Abba, could you open the floor at the bottom of the closet? Could you? Could you? Please? It's very important for a school report thing I need! Quick!" I pointed to the bottom of the closet. "That!"

He chuckled. He said, "You esk Mommy? Vat she said?"

"Mommy?" I asked. "She's busy." And I begged and pleaded and promised that I would take real good care of him when he got old.

But my father refused. Without my mother's permission, he couldn't, he shouldn't, he just vouldn't. He had built the study and the closet just for her. He had reconstructed the entire space, closing up the back door, putting in the closet and shelves—enough to make room for the entire Holocaust—and adding three windows to let in the sun. He looked proudly around as he said this.

I stood, glum, my arms crossed angrily over my chest. I stared ahead. The secret door, please.

My father looked down at me. He said that if my grouch grew any grouchier, my cheeks would fall right off.

I pouted harder than ever.

Then I heard the front door. My mother was back.

Later that evening, I asked Rivky if she knew about the secret place under the closet, but she said it was none of my business. I asked her if she knew what was in there, besides the Holocaust, but again she said, "If Mommy said not to look, then you are not allowed to look."

I went to Yitzy. He said there were important things in there, and he knew exactly what, but he couldn't tell. And that he had once opened the closet floor and had gotten a ringing slap across his face.

Finally I thought: Nachum. I would show him the secret door. He would certainly open it and take everything out. Then I could blame him for the trouble.

But Nachum got trapped under a falling wardrobe before I could even try. When it fell right on top of his body, he didn't make a sound. We only knew something had happened because we heard a loud crash from down the hall. Then silence.

My mother rushed out of the kitchen. My father came running after her. They found Nachum in my room lying trapped under the wardrobe where I kept my clothes, only his head sticking out, his eyes staring at a point on the wall. He blinked heavily. His lips did not move. It was as if the pain had not reached him yet, as if his brain did not know that a large piece of furniture had pinned him down.

My father lifted the wardrobe off him and Nachum jumped up like a caged animal let loose. My mother reached out to him. She said, "Nachum, Nachum, show me where you hurt yourself! Show me! What happened?" But my brother rushed past her, his head jerking forward, his left cheek protruding as he anxiously bit the side of his tongue.

If a wardrobe had fallen on me, pinning my body to the floor, the only way I wouldn't have shrieked loud enough that they'd hear me all the way to Heaven was if I were dead. But my brother was alive, with eyes that looked but could not see, ears that worked but didn't hear, and skin that touched but did not feel—not the cold of the snow, not the warmth of my mother's arms, not the slamming of an armoire against his small body. Yet if you tried to hug him, he jumped as if he'd been scorched by fire. He felt too much, or not at all. He was like a prisoner wrongfully jailed, and he kept knocking his head against the ground, begging to be let out.

Later, after the doctor left, I saw my father enter Nachum's room. My brother was curled up on his bed, eyes shut, swaying back and forth like a pendulum, his head banging into the mattress springs, maybe looking for a way inside, into his strange, walled-off world. My father stared down at my brother, his mouth grim beneath his mustache, his eyes like dark tunnels.

Back. Forth.
Back. Forth.
Back. Forth.
Back...

And this after he'd been home for three weeks, attending the special Chush school that was to cure him.

It was the next day that I made my second deal with God.

Ten

Friday is a terrible time to make a deal with God. It is a busy time, only half a day, really, with Shabbos coming at sundown, and all the work to be done beforehand.

On Friday, we had only three hours of school. By noon, we were dismissed, sent home to help our mothers prepare. The Friday of my failed deal with God began no differently than the others. I sat in the blanket box at the head of my bed, hiding from my mother and the chores I did not want to do. I was preparing myself for a meaningful conversation with God.

There was no time to waste. I folded my legs so that I was comfortable. I carefully covered my knees with my uniform skirt, so as not to be immodest. Then, with my hands spread out like a prayer book, I eased my way into my heavenly request. I explained to God that I wanted to do the fast thing, the forty-days-and-nights thing, the way I'd done for the earrings back when He had made me that miracle.

I thought things were going well. I was pleading and

promising extra psalms, but this time God got mad. Suddenly, everything went dark. I was buried in shadows and could not see a thing.

"Help!" I screamed. "Help!" I pushed at the suffocating darkness until there was light again. I blinked in the brightness, my head sticking out from under two heavy blankets, and found myself looking up at my sister, the one who'd thrown the quilts inside without bothering to check first.

Rivky stared down at me in surprise.

"What are you doing in the blanket box?"

I pushed the blankets away. "You buried me alive!" I yelled angrily. "And it's none of your business! Get out!"

My sister stomped away. "You have to set the table for the Shabbos meal!" she shouted.

I shoved the blankets out of the box and sat down again. I leaned back, ready to start whispering fervently to God. But then, just as I began, I heard my mother's voice.

"*Me-nu*-chah!"

I could tell that she was angry.

"Come now!"

That meant now.

I threw up my hands, exasperated. Did they not know what I was doing? I banged my fist against the side of the box.

"I'm praying!" I screeched.

There was quiet. I took a deep breath, sighed, and started again. My mother's puzzled face peered in at me. Wisps of red hair stuck out from under her kerchief. There were smudges of white flour on her housecoat.

"You're what?" she asked.

I thought of explaining. Then I thought better of it. I stared back at her silently.

She shook her head impatiently. "Where do you think you are—a hotel? Shabbos is in three hours! You don't sit in a box now! Come peel the potatoes! And make sure you turn off the oven in an hour or the kugel will burn."

The phone rang. She hurried away. The smell of sweet lokshen kugel wafted into my room, right through the walls, and into my prayers. I sighed and gestured to the heavens. This was terrible timing.

There was a sudden roar from the kitchen as the mixer turned on. The beaters whirred loudly, turning gooey egg whites into frothy snow. My mother was baking the Shabbos cake, the vanilla sponge kind that was my most favorite thing.

I jumped up and finished with God.

"Dear, dear God," I said hurriedly. "If I fast for forty days and nights, please do a miracle and make my brother normal."

I said this three times just in case, so it would be as clear as possible, and also because I was in a rush. I wanted leftover cake batter before my sister got her hands on it.

Shabbos was getting closer.

"Try on the Shabbos robe I bought you," my mother called. I grabbed the robe on my mother's bed. It fit. Good. I took it off and tossed it on the floor.

"And don't leave the robe on the floor!"

I picked up the robe.

I set the dining room table. Then I stuck my face inside the flat container of gefilte fish and ate. My mother demanded that I take my face out of her gefilte fish; she had worked on it all night long.

Only an hour and a half to Shabbos.

It was nearly dusk, but my father wasn't home. It was the traffic again. And no matter how many times my mother had told him not to be late for Sabbath! No matter how many times... Why couldn't the man leave earlier?

My little sister, Miri, refused to take a bath. And my sister Rivky called me a rotten brat because I refused to move the gefilte fish from the pot to the plastic container. But in with the fish was an actual fish's head, beady dead eyes and hollow skull, and I said I was not going to touch it. I'd throw up if I had to—I would. Yitzy said that I was a real baby, because once upon a time in Jerusalem (Aunt Tziporah always said), our grandmother brought home a live fish every Thursday night and put it in the bathtub to swim. On Shabbos eve, she'd take it out and hold it down on the kitchen counter. Then, with the words *"L'kovod Shabbos kodesh"*—in honor of the holy Shabbos—she'd clop the thing over the head with the wooden clopper, praying for its quick death.

Sometimes the fish would slip out of my grandmother's hands and Tziporah and her brothers would run around the kitchen in circles, screeching, as the fish, in honor of the holy

71

Shabbos, jumped and flapped on the hard stone floor and my grandmother chased after it, clopper in hand.

And I couldn't move one fish head from pot to plastic container.

I told Yitzy that I lived in New York. And I wasn't touching the head of any dead fish, not for a hundred dollars.

Shabbos was in a half hour. My mother ordered me to call my father—now!

I picked up the receiver to call his car phone. I dialed— just as the front door swung open. It was my father. "It's thirty minutes to Shabbos!" I hollered into the phone anyway. "Why couldn't you leave *earlier?*"

Twenty minutes to Shabbos.

My mother rushed out of the bathroom. My father rushed in. I rushed around, just because. Miri spilled strawberry yogurt all over her new Shabbos robe.

A neighbor came by. She needed the eggs I had borrowed last week. We did not have any eggs. She said I was irresponsible.

Ten minutes.

Mrs. Meitelis called. I picked up the phone. She said there

was a Shabbos *kallah* after lunch tomorrow celebrating her daughter's engagement. My mother should come. "Make sure you give her the message, Menuchah, okay?" Not like last time, when I had forgotten to give the message until Sunday evening. I was totally, incorrigibly scatterbrained. "Okay," I said. "Mazel tov and *gut Shabbos*."

Five minutes.

The shower was turned off. The garbage had been taken out. The lights in the dining room switched on. My father, his beard glistening, walked swiftly into the room. He set eight small candlesticks on the silver candelabra and the long silver candlelighter near it. Then he pulled on his long Shabbos overcoat. He took out his *shtreimel* and set it carefully on his head.

"Gut Shabbos," he called out. "You have four minutes left!"

My father gave me a kiss on the forehead. Also one on the nose. Then he and Yitzy went off to shul.

I stood on the couch, my face pressed against the window, watching them walk down the block. I thought my father looked like a king, with the *shtreimel* like a crown on his head. I watched the fur hat moving regally along, growing smaller and smaller, until it was gone.

I looked up at the heavens. The sun spread majestically in the sky, streaks of red and orange stretching wide along the horizon like shimmering ribbons. Then, as a streak of red dipped and bowed, touching the roof of a distant building, the low wailing of the Shabbos siren rose over the Brooklyn neighborhood, announcing to all Jews everywhere that the before time was over. Shabbos had come.

My mother stood by the candelabra in her elegant velvet Shabbos robe and held the candlelighter. Pointing the lighter at the wicks, she tapped them gently, one by one, as if with a magic wand, and eight flickering flames jumped to life. They danced under the glow of the chandelier, near the sparkling silver kiddush cup and covered challah bread. The warm aroma of chicken soup swirled slowly into the living room.

My mother swayed. She recited the blessing over the candles. She raised her hands, circling the candelabra three times, ushering in the Shabbos queen. Then she covered her eyes and prayed.

Once, long ago, in the days of the shtetl in Europe, the great rebbe of Viloshnik said that the words uttered over the Shabbos candlelight hold the power of many prayers. He said that the holy mitzvah of the Shabbos candles could undo any curse from above, and any sins from a dark past. Each time a woman asks for her sons to grow up to become Torah scholars, for her daughters to be future mothers of the nation of Israel, the angels dance with joy. And God is happy.

My mother's hands trembled. Her face was hidden beneath the palms of her hands. I could not hear her words, but I could hear her tears. She wept quietly. She was asking God for a miracle.

Miri ran into the dining room, holding Avrumi's stuffed rabbit. Vrumi chased angrily after her. Still, my mother prayed. Rivky sat in the chair near the flames, her siddur open to the Friday night L'cha Dodi prayer. I folded napkins into sailboats and airplanes.

Finally, my mother finished. She uncovered her face and stared wistfully at the flames. She wiped her eyes and looked down at us.

"*Gut Shabbos,*" she said quietly and then smiled.

Then she saw Nachum, standing like a stranger at the entrance to the dining room. He was staring at the flames of the holy Shabbos candles, hypnotized. My mother walked toward him. Her hands reached out, beckoning him, but Nachum never saw her. She bent down, pulling him into her arms, and he stared at the flames over her shoulder. He could not feel my mother's embrace. He did not know he was being held.

My mother kissed Nachum on the forehead. She hugged him quickly, and then he pulled away.

I wondered about my ancestors. Why, if there were so many of them, noble rabbis and holy saints, had they not already made a miracle? After all, wasn't it my own great-great-grand-father, the Vunder Rebbe, who did just that for so many others? Then why not for us?

My teacher had once told us that when a person prays from his heart, all of Heaven hears his desperation. The souls of our ancestors carry those prayers aloft, ensuring that they reach the heavenly throne. Then, standing in front of the Almighty Himself, they pray on our behalf.

So what was happening up there? I could not understand.

It was really impossible to know. Because my teacher also said that in Heaven, at times, there can be a *stiah*, an obstruction, a spirit blocking the heartfelt prayer. Sometimes it is a sin from the past, long forgotten; sometimes it's a soul with a grudge from the days he was on earth that can keep a plea from reaching its destination. And God is deaf to such prayers. To have a *stiah* is to be cursed.

Eleven

In the city of Jerusalem, there were two sides: the one where the rich lived, and the one filled with the poor. My father lived on the poor side. He lived there with his four siblings, the alley cats, and a father who was crippled in both body and head.

That's why there were no pictures of my father when he was a little boy, said my mother. That's why there were no pictures of his sisters in elegant, frilly clothes. Because my father grew up in a one-bedroom apartment by the border, where only the poorest lived, right near where the Jordanian soldiers guarded their side of Jerusalem.

Things hadn't always been that way. Once, my father's father, Sabah Mechel, had been a healthy man. Once, my grandmother Savtah Liba had been happy. Perhaps they were poor, with five children in a tiny home, but no one was ever hungry. There were chicken legs for soup, warm socks from the *shuk* for the feet, and Aunt Dina, Sabah

Mechel's sister, from around the corner, who sent cakes and little snacks.

My grandmother Savtah Liba had suffered endlessly in her life. She had survived Auschwitz, watching her entire family turned to ash. Then, in the refugee camp, only one year after the war, she lost her new husband. When she arrived in Israel in 1947, she was alone, with a toddler by her side and a new-born in her arms.

Two years later, Savtah Liba married my grandfather Sabah Mechel, a milkman. They were poor, even very poor, for how much did a milkman earn? But my grandmother was happier than she had ever been because Sabah Mechel was a kind and generous soul who treated his wife like a queen.

Sabah Mechel polished my grandmother's shoes every Friday until they shone like new, in honor of the holy Shabbos. Sabah Mechel bought my Savtah Liba pretty trinkets, a brooch for her dress, a shawl for the cold, a hat that matched her eyes. Sabah Mechel helped keep the house clean—not an easy job, what with the mopping, and the laundry, and the heavy metal pots. And one day, he came home with an expensive new vegetable peeler, made in the faraway land of America.

On Friday nights, in the synagogue, Sabah Mechel gave candies to children who prayed with fervor, and sometimes, at the Shabbos meal, he'd give the food off his own dinner plate to beggars passing by, because they were still poorer than him.

Sabah Mechel worked hard to earn a living, rising each morning before the sun. He'd wheel the milk wagon to the corner of the main street, unload a large metal canister from the dairy truck, a thirty-pound barrel filled with milk from the kibbutz farms. Sabah Mechel would hoist the canister onto the wagon, which he pushed through crisscrossing lanes, over cobblestones and dirt streets. He would hum a *nigun* to himself as he filled the glass bottles that stood patiently beside closed doors with fresh, white milk. At eight, when the sun shone bright in the sky, he parked his milk wagon and went off to morning prayers.

Down the main hallway from where my father's family lived was the bathroom they shared with the Rosens. Also with the Yuds, the Klaynmans, and the Itamars. Mostly, the families got along and there was peace and harmony. Here and there, a problem arose, like when the Klaynmans got diarrhea, all eight of them at once, or when Little Mendel stuffed his socks down the toilet, blocking the drain completely.

Mendel was my father's youngest brother, and he had never meant to block the drain completely. In fact, as soon as the socks disappeared into the darkness of the bowl, Mendel changed his mind. He wanted his socks back, to pull up over his cold feet, but it was too late. They were already stuck.

So Mendel called my father, Shloimy, then seven years old, who grabbed a broom from outside the Itamars' door and thumped it down the drain. Mendel locked the bathroom so the neighbors could not see as his older brother pulled and pushed, pushed and pulled at the socks that would not budge from deep inside the toilet. Mendel said two psalms for unplugging the toilet, the way he'd done to heal his stray cat, and it was then, as my father gave a final push, that the socks came spurting up—along with everything else.

Shloimy told Mendel to stop praying. Now was the time to flee.

They dropped the broom on the overflowing bathroom floor and ran to the courtyard, where they started playing *kugelach* and tag as if they'd been there all afternoon, never once looking back. They chased cats down the alley and dared each other to touch the entrance door of the dark building where the Christian missionaries lived, those who kidnapped Jewish orphans.

When Mr. Itamar returned home to the screams of his wife, hovering over her filth-caked broom, he grabbed his sons, each by one ear, demanding to know which of the little fools had stuffed the only toilet with his socks. They yelped and screamed and said they didn't know, but Mr. Itamar made them clean up the mess anyway while my father and Mendel sat several courtyards away eating Aunt Dina's cakes and snacks.

Life could have gone on like this forever, but it didn't. Perhaps because God saw that things were better for Savtah Liba and He got worried. She had already been happy for several years.

So it was a rather simple thing for an angel to trip Sabah Mechel in the dark, to send him stumbling down the stone steps with his wagon, and to see to it that his head hit the sharp edge of a brick or stone. The milk, rushing from the overturned canister, streamed down the street, all wasted, but Sabah Mechel never noticed. Blood covered his eyes, soaking the fallen *kippa* near his head, red mixing with white, as the wheels of the wagon spun in the dark, silent air of Jerusalem.

It was Yanofsky who saw him first as he walked down the street on his way to early morning prayers. Yanofsky dragged Sabah Mechel to the hospital, where they stopped the bleeding, wrapping his head in gauze and plaster. But Sabah Mechel did not open his eyes for days. In the operating room, a surgeon with a sharp knife cut open the back of Sabah Mechel's head and poked around worriedly inside. Then, finding nothing but smashed skull, he sewed Sabah Mechel back together again with a needle, a thread, and a prayer.

Sabah Mechel was discharged several weeks later. There was nothing more the doctors could do. The ambulance brought him home, and he lay in the apartment's one bedroom in crippling pain. He was a generous soul still, but now there was a raging violence that burst randomly from the cracks of his broken skull, and it was impossible to know what would set it off.

Sabah Mechel could no longer wake up at dawn, so Savtah Liba went to work instead. She rose each morning before the sun, pushing the milk wagon down the twisting lanes.

Sabah Mechel's seventy-five-year-old mother, Bubba Tzirah, moved in to care for her crippled son. In the morning, she filled the house with the smell of cheese strudel and fresh bread. In the evening, she cooked warm soup and scrubbed the little ones clean. Sometimes she sent Hadassah, the oldest, to help her mother with the milk at dawn. Sometimes she sent my father, already eight years old and strong enough, to help too. They filled glass bottles as the sun rose over the city, and children rushed past them to school. Some mornings, Hadassah would see her teacher walking hurriedly down the street. Crouching behind a gate or a wall, she hid until the teacher was gone and could not see her poverty and shame.

Things got better when Savtah Liba found a job koshering chickens in the butcher's store. There she did not need to wake up before the sun. There no one could see her, standing in bloodstained clothes in the refrigerated back room, salting crates of headless chickens until every speck of blood was drawn out and the meat was kosher and pure, and the skin had come off the palms of both of her hands.

But the butcher was a good man. He gave Savtah Liba drumsticks and chicken breasts to take home to her children free of charge.

"We were poor, I guess," Aunt Tziporah would say. "But we never thought about it. Everyone was poor. Sometimes when there was some extra money, we bought wafer crumbs at the *shuk*. They were sold at the kiosk, right near the licorice and chocolate and things we couldn't afford. The wafer crumbs were delicious. There were two boxes of them, one filled with vanilla crumbs, the other with chocolate crumbs, and for only a shekel we could fill half a bag."

So who complained? Nobody ever complained, and Savtah Liba kept her suffering to herself. Because in the city of Jerusalem there were two sides: the one where the rich lived, and the one filled with the poor. My father lived among the poor—there, with his siblings and his crippled father; there, amidst suffering and illness; there, where the alley cats yowled of their hunger and were chased down ancient lanes by the hiss of old men's shoes. God's earth was hard enough. Nobody was interested in hearing about the general suffering too.

Twelve

A decade and a half later, in New York, my father, already grown and married to my mother, became almost a millionaire.

My father worked hard in Brooklyn, where he and his sisters moved just as soon as they could. He rolled matzos in the bakery, cut diamonds in Manhattan, and bought houses for cheap to fix and sell. You could do this in America, he said to me, step off the plane with only the shirt on your back and become a wealthy man.

I asked my father if he had a million dollars, and he said almost, in just a little more time. I told him that I knew we were rich because Blimi had said so. She said that I was the wealthiest of the girls in my class because I had a white house three stories high, and two cars besides, one of them with doors that opened automatically. She also said that I had the biggest backyard she'd ever seen, and that only rich people had a wraparound garden like ours.

My father said that money was an important thing to have, even if it was less than a million dollars. With money, he could buy us the things he'd never had. With money, a man could repair anything, patch it up or buy it new. He could fix problems that, without money, stayed problems, like the chipped tooth in Rivky's mouth, Yitzy's bike that crashed into a tree, the dented car.

But then there were the things my father could not fix, not even with his money: the sunrise I'd meticulously drawn and Miri had shredded; the antique radio we had found, decades old, that would not work; and my crazy brother Nachum, now seven years old. My father paid psychologists, doctors, and special teachers, but nobody could fix the boy. They could not even figure out why or how he was broken.

Long before, when my brother was two and three, my mother had thought that he'd grow out of it, that time would fix his strange ways. But then my brother turned four and five and things only got worse, especially in school. In the end, it was his pre-1-A rebbe, Reb Gold, who called my mother. It was he who finally told her that Nachum was crazy, that the parts inside his head were undone.

Reb Gold hadn't said it like that. He said that Nachum was different. Nachum wasn't listening. He was throwing chairs at the other children. He said that Nachum wasn't hearing. He had stopped speaking. He made strange noises and faces.

Reb Gold was a good man. He said all this to my mother kindly, telling her that this was more than just strange, that Nachum must be taken for testing. So my mother took my brother from doctor to doctor, and from one specialist to another. She took him to a psychiatrist, a psychologist, and a hypnotist too; it couldn't hurt.

The specialist told my mother to put Nachum in an institution. There was nothing anyone could do for a child as odd as that. The psychiatrist said that something was definitely terribly wrong with Nachum and that it was my mother's fault: when he was an infant, she had not cuddled him enough. The doctor said that something had almost certainly happened to Nachum during the pregnancy. Or as an infant. Or as a toddler. But he couldn't know when or what. And the psychologist said that it was tragic, just tragic.

Finally, one day, my mother told me that my brother wasn't crazy after all. A big doctor had said he was something else. He was ADD. The severe kind.

I told my cousin Shaindel.

"What's ADD?" she asked.

I didn't know.

"It's a type of crazy," I explained. "The severe kind."

Shaindel chewed loudly on her taffy. "Oh."

I asked my mother if medicine would make Nachum better. Or, if they couldn't change his brain, could they replace it? The way they had put a different heart into Blimi's grandmother.

"No, they can't."

That was all she said.

My father did not like that Nachum could not be fixed. He did not like what the angel had done, tap, tap, tapping on my unborn brother's lip until he had sucked up his mind. My father did not like the special school that could not cure him, or the teachers who had no idea what to do. One evening, he and my mother had a fight in the kitchen, about Nachum and the experts and whether there was hope.

I wanted to tell them about the tapping angel, because they didn't know. But I was scared of their yelling—I'd never heard them like this before—and instead hid deep inside my blanket. My father shouted, my mother screamed back; then she cried. She said hers was not a hopeless child. I put my hands over my ears.

The next week, after another such fight, my mother took us all to a family psychologist who said we should talk about our feelings. But my father didn't like him either.

"So tell me how you feel," the psychologist instructed him, after my parents had sat on the couch and my siblings and I had squished ourselves into little plastic chairs.

"Ken you fix my son?" my father asked.

The psychologist peered over his half-glasses.

"I can't fix your son," he said. "But I can try to fix the feelings you have about your son—"

"No, you ken't," said my brave father. "You ever hev such a son?"

"No," said the psychologist. "I have not."

My father tapped his fingers on the armrest.

"Zen you ken't fix my feel about vat you don' even know."

The psychologist pushed the half-glasses up the bridge of his nose. My father stood up from the couch.

"I don' look for change in feeling. I look only for change in son." The psychologist shook his head and opened his mouth to say something. But my father did not wait.

"You don' vaste my time," he said, and walked out of the office, closing the door behind him.

I wanted to run out of the office too. I wanted to march out with my father, tall, proud, and mad. I wanted to declare to the world and the stupid psychologist that I didn't care how I felt about my brother, and that they could not keep me, squirming and squished, in a hard little plastic chair. Nachum was the one who was broken. So why was I the one stuck here?

It was my mother who made me stay. She made me sit and say how I felt to the man and his stupid half-glasses.

Thirteen

It was December, the day after Chanukah. Outside, bare trees wrapped themselves in snow, their white-covered branches flailing frantically in the wind.

In the kitchen, the cleaning lady was polishing my father's silver menorah, the one he had lit for eight nights. On the counter nearby stood Yitzy's smaller menorah, the one he'd received at his birthday. My sisters and I also had menorahs, ones we had made in school, flatter, smaller, and more color-ful, crusted with the wax of melting candles, from flames that had flickered at the frosted windows of our dining room.

The menorahs now stood patiently on the kitchen counter, waiting to be polished and cleaned. They waited to be carried back to the dining room to be carefully placed behind the glass panes of the closet, where they'd stand alongside the rest of the family silver until next year.

On Thursday evening, the last night of Chanukah, I had run upstairs to Kathy and given her a doughnut. It was a good doughnut from Weiss's bakery, with frosting on top and custard inside. Kathy said that I was making her fat, but she ate the entire doughnut happily. I stayed with her for just a few minutes and then quickly ran back down, so I did not realize until the next evening, after my mother had already lit the Shabbos candles, that I'd left my schoolbag with my favorite Hello Kitty eraser and my homework sheet upstairs.

I looked carefully around me. Rivky was reading a book on the couch. My mother was in the kitchen talking with my great-aunt, who was visiting from Israel. Little Miri and Vrumi were playing in the basement. I walked quietly to the front door. Once out, I rushed upstairs and immediately back down, the only problem being the in-between, when I spoke with Kathy for a really long time.

I did not realize just how long a time. I only knew I was in trouble when I skipped merrily down the steps to the first floor and found Rivky waiting at the bottom, hand on hip, her patent leather shoe tapping righteously on the floor. It was one thing to visit a gentile on any school day, she said, but on the holy Shabbos?

Rivky pursed her lips. "We're ready to eat," she said loudly. "And I'm going to tell everyone exactly where you went."

I stared at my sister in horror. I immediately explained that I had gone to get my school *parsha* sheet, the one with questions about the weekly Torah portion that I needed to review on the holy Shabbos itself.

"Oh yeah?" she said. "So where is it?"

I looked down at my empty hands. Where was the *parsha*

sheet? Between the up and down and the in-between, I had completely forgotten it. Now I looked like a liar.

"It was a necessary sin," I explained hastily. "It was all for the sake of Shabbos. I had to go up to Kathy for the *parsha* sheet but she didn't have it because she mistakenly threw it out with my Hello Kitty eraser. So it isn't my fault, 'cause she was looking for it and I was helping her, 'cause I didn't want to leave a holy *parsha* sheet with a gentile. That'd be terrible for the honor of Shabbos. And anyway, I need to be friends with Kathy. She's gonna save me when a new Holocaust comes."

I took a deep breath. "Okay?"

Rivky looked at me without speaking. I could see in her eyes that she thought I was making it all up.

I stuck out my tongue. She spun around and marched toward the dining room. I ran after her.

"Don't tell," I hissed into her ear. "Don't tell! If you do, I'll...I'll...I'll—" And then I nearly crashed into my great-aunt Frieda, here for the Friday night meal.

I did not like my great-aunt Frieda. She was old and small and gave terribly wet kisses. But Aunt Frieda was the wife of Mordcha', my grandmother's only surviving brother, so I had no choice but to treat her nicely. She had come to America for a two-week visit, and my mother had warmly invited her for the Shabbos dinner.

Aunt Frieda loved my mother, her youngest and favorite niece.

"Esther!" she had exclaimed happily when my mother opened the door before Shabbos. "Look at you! As pretty as the day you finally became a bride!"

I stood the farthest away, but she came at me first. She held my cheeks in her hands and squeezed. She kissed me four times, twice on the right, then on the left, her stiff, curly wig scratching my skin. She patted my face, pinched my chin, and said, "What a beautiful girl! What a beautiful girl!" I wiped my face on my sleeve.

"Ahh," Aunt Frieda said, sighing contentedly and seating herself at the head of the table. "Such beautiful children. Such beautiful children. When did they all grow up?"

She pointed at Rivky.

"Look at that face," she announced cheerfully. "Now that's a Jewish face!" She waved her hand emphatically. "Eh! She would never survive the Holocaust."

She stroked Rivky's arm to reassure her.

My mother smiled lovingly. She thought we were beautiful too, not that it mattered. Beauty was a superficial thing for the goyish world. Here, for us, there were only two kinds of faces that mattered: those that would survive the Holocaust, and those that would not. My mother, sitting across the Shabbos table, studied us one by one. She agreed that Rivky would never have made it through the war. She was all dark hair and large Jewish eyes.

"But who knows?" my aunt said enthusiastically. "Who but the one above knows? Your own mother with her dark eyes is alive and well, and her oldest brother—he looked like an Aryan thug! He was killed. Nothing remained of him."

They looked at Rivky again. They then agreed once more that regardless of God, should the Nazis come, Rivky was doomed.

My brother Yitzy, on the other hand, would stroll right through. He and Miri, my baby sister, were blond with blue eyes and freckles. They could easily pass for German or at least a good Polish. Why, they'd barely need a place to hide.

And as for me, well...I was a puzzle, a great big puzzle.

My great-aunt observed me up close. My mother pursed her lips, pondering. I was not blond nor black-haired. I was not blue- nor brown-eyed. I was not particularly fair, but not very dark either. This left me in a confusing place, somewhere between Jewish and gentile, life and death, the right and left of Dr. Mengele's long stick.

Aunt Frieda squinted and peered at me. I smiled hopefully. I turned sideways so she could see the one dimple I had on my right cheek. Because there was no way I was not surviving the Holocaust while my bratty little sister just skipped right through. Then, just as Aunt Frieda was to announce my final chance for life should a new Holocaust come, Nachum walked in. She turned abruptly.

"Nachum!" she said, clapping her hands. He looked up, startled.

I cleared my throat loudly, but they had already forgotten me.

It was all very annoying. Nobody ever seemed to make up their minds whether I would or would not survive a Holocaust. Just what was I to *do* when the Nazis showed up?

Well, there was always Kathy, I supposed. She could hide me. I could take shelter under her coffee table until the war was over, eating lettuce, raw potatoes, and saltless crackers. But even that was uncertain. Everyone always said that one should not trust the gentiles—any gentile; that even those who seemed to be our friends would hand us over to the Nazis for only one bottle of vodka and three bags of sugar. All gentiles were nice, my teachers said, until there was a Holocaust, and then their evilness sprouted right out.

This worried me. I tried to find the evilness and where it might sprout out from every time I went to visit Kathy, but I could not find a hint of it anywhere.

Just then my aunt laughed. "Look at that smile!" she said victoriously. "Of course he'll survive!"

I looked up. Crazy Nachum had only smiled, and already he'd survive the next great massacre?

It was the dimples. He had two of them. My aunt had put a small prize in his hand, and he had flashed a bright smile. When Nachum smiled, a dimple appeared on each cheek that even some annoying neighbor had once said was adorable.

I could not believe it. So Nachum would survive the Holocaust, while I, of uncertain classification, would be stuck in a cramped attic apartment?

I stared woefully at my gefilte fish and kicked the table. My mother never noticed. Neither did my older sister. She was piling up the first-course plates, taking them to the kitchen. My father was teasing Miri, plucking her thumb out of her mouth every time she tried sucking on it. With his other hand, he held on to Vrumi, bouncing him on his knees. And my mother, she just laughed, was already talking about something else, a dress my great-aunt had bought two sizes too small.

Then my father and older brother sang the holy Shabbos songs and my great-aunt Frieda sang along loudly. She smiled blissfully at me, her head moving to the beat, her hands waving two silver spoons in the air, as if she were conducting an orchestra. I could hear Rivky giggling helplessly in the kitchen.

I scowled, and when my mother asked me to help clear the rest of the plates, I refused.

"Rivky said she'd do it," I lied.

Bossy older sister. She would never have survived the Holocaust anyway. See if I cared.

Fourteen

When my father was nine years old, he found his Bubba Tzirah dead in the bed they shared. My father thought it was strange that his grandmother was still sleeping, because Bubba Tzirah always woke with the sun. She would turn on the fire under the stove and knead the dough for fresh bread, always murmuring the words of the psalms by heart. But one morning, Bubba Tzirah would not wake up. My father pulled her hand and called her name. His brother Zev jumped on the bed, chanting in his high-pitched voice, "Bubba Tzirah, wake up! Bubba Tzirah, wake up! The cat drank up the milk!," because there was no breakfast on the table, no warm smells from the kitchen, and he was hungry.

It was Sabah Mechel who opened his eyes in the other room. He got up and shuffled to their bed, gesturing angrily. He hovered over his mother, the dark scar visible on his scalp. When he saw her still, unmoving form, devoid of life or breath, Sabah Mechel screamed to the heavens, shouting the prayers for the dead.

A kindly neighbor ran to tell Savtah Liba of her mother-in-law's death, because Savtah Liba no longer lived with her husband. Two years after the angel had turned him into a raging cripple, my grandmother moved out. She took the girls and her youngest child, Mendel, to an apartment a few blocks away. Savtah Liba did this silently and without complaint, after my grandfather beat Mendel for skipping and singing around the table. Then he lovingly shined her shoes for the holy Shabbos. Then he threw the dishes across the room, missing her by barely an inch.

My father and his brother Zev stayed with Bubba Tzirah and their broken father because their mother could not care for them alone. Perhaps with only his elder sons and his mother to cook and clean, Sabah Mechel would care for the boys the way he used to.

After she left Sabah Mechel, he bent his broken body and wept. He sent the boys to bring pots and pans and little trinkets to Savtah Liba's new apartment. He thought she might still decide to come back.

But Savtah Liba never did. Sometimes she sent Tziporah to check on her brothers, to look through the window from the outside and see what was happening. Tziporah obeyed. She walked down the streets to her father's home and looked through the window, but when she came back, she lied. She said that things were good there and quiet. She never told her mother about the terrible beatings. She never told her about the belt, how it swung high in the air, up and down, up and down, as Sabah Mechel went after Shloimy and Zev, slashing the strip of leather against their backs and thighs until he was too exhausted to go on.

After Bubba Tzirah's death, my father and his brother were sent to an orphanage. There they were hit with sticks. There my father ate apple peels from the garbage behind the kitchen because he was hungry and the peels tasted fresh and good. From there he ran away three times, until they got tired of bringing him back.

After less than a year, my father and his brother Zev moved back in with their mother in the other apartment. It had two bedrooms, which was more than one, and somehow they found space. Every Sabbath and holiday they'd visit their father at the apartment near the border—until the day his body gave out.

Perhaps the angel who had tripped him looked down from Heaven and pitied him for his suffering. Perhaps he pleaded with God, begging for His mercy, to release the pious Jew from his agony. For weeks Sabah Mechel lay in the hospital, between the living and the dead, waiting for the Almighty to make up His merciful mind. Finally, a few weeks after Chanukah, as the wind and cold blew through the cities and hills of the Holy Land, the Lord nodded. Up in Heaven, the angel of death spread his powerful wings. Then he flew downward, toward Jerusalem.

It was the end of February, seven days after my father's bar mitzvah, and five years after the accident, when Sabah Mechel's generous soul departed from his broken body. At the hospital, ten men stood around the bed and chanted prayers for the dead. At the cemetery in the high hills outside Jerusalem, the brothers and sisters watched as men carried their father's body, wrapped in a prayer shawl, to the open grave. They laid Sabah Mechel gently down. Then they covered him with spadefuls of earth.

Stones and pebbles, and the plainest of headstones announced his name and years on earth: Sabah Mechel, 1906–1965, a father, a husband, a pious Jew, "may his soul be bound up in the bond of eternal life."

It was twenty years after the Holocaust. Israel was still healing. Between the wars of the present and the dead of the past, there was simply no room for more tragedy. The poor and the ill would just have to make do. This was not a good time to be a fatherless child.

Part II

Fifteen

My teacher, Mrs. Friedman, said that fairy tales were un-kosher. They were silly stories filled with immorality: Goldi-locks who stole the porridge, the wolf who blew down a house that was not his, and the princesses, all of them, who dressed immodestly and fell in love.

"We have beautiful, uplifting stories of our own," she said, "of sages and saints and miracles. We don't need the goyim's schmutz."

I did not tell Mrs. Friedman that my mother had taken me a few weeks earlier to Manhattan, where she had bought me a real fairy-tale book. It had been right before Chanukah and snow-ing outside. There were ice puddles and mounds of snow as tall as I was on the sidewalks and corners of Brooklyn, and white garbage trucks rolled down the streets, clearing paths for cars.

Outside, in our garden, Yitzy, Rivky, and I had built a snowman with a shawl around its neck to keep it warm. Yitzy put an old black *kippa* on its head, but it kept tumbling off. It was hard to be both snowman and Jew.

That week, I had promised my mother that I would do well in school, and somehow I had. So on Monday, after the weekend, she picked me up early and we took the train to the city, just my mother and me.

"To a big bookstore," she told me. "The largest one you've ever seen..."

And it's true that I had never been in such a bookstore before, with its high ceilings, enormous windows, and an entire floor just for children. Colorful signs hung from the lights, cardboard cutouts of Winnie-the-Pooh, Big Bird, and a knight on a flying horse.

My mother said that I should look around carefully. She would buy me whichever book I chose.

I looked at Sesame Street books, and *Ramona Quimby, Age 8*, and the Happy Hollisters in the haunted house. I looked at mystery books, adventure books, and books about faraway places. Then I reached the bookshelves under the flying horse. Right near it were low, round tables with small chairs where children could sit and read. On one table was a pile of books and a toddler trying to eat them. He screamed as his mother pulled him away, and he kicked at the pile, which fell to the floor. I picked up the books. That's when I saw the fairy-tale book, larger than the others, gleaming with colors and magic.

The Enchanted Book of Fairy Tales had two princesses on the cover. Green ivy leaves twisted wildly on the castle behind them and down the borders of the book. The princesses wore pink hats, beautiful lace sashes sweeping from their tops. They wore sparkling gowns and pointy, silken shoes on their feet. One held an open scroll, the other a silver magic wand.

I sat down on the floor by the table and began to read.

The Enchanted Book of Fairy Tales said, "Once upon a time there was a princess," "Once upon a time there was a prince," and "Once upon a time there was an evil queen." The princesses were beautiful and slender, the princes handsome and strong, the queens red-faced and angry. There were fairies and spells, there were goblins and bearded dwarfs, and they all knew how to do magic. Then, when they were done, everyone lived happily ever after.

My mother's nose twitched ever so slightly when I showed her this book. She turned the pages. Her finger hovered questioningly over the roaring beast, the cackling mouth of the witch. Then she closed the book and held out a smaller one, about a girl in pigtails.

"Look," she said, smiling. "It's a girl your age!"

But I didn't like pigtails on girls my age, or on anyone. I shook my head.

My mother held out another book. It was about a boy with a mystery to solve. "Yitzy loves this book. It's exciting. He read it twice."

I looked at the ceiling. Stupid book.

"This one?" She offered another.

I scowled.

"This one," she commanded.

I tapped my foot. Nope.

"Oh, and look at this one." There were flying red balloons on the cover and a man in a hat.

I held the book of fairy tales close to my heart. This one.

My mother sighed. "Are you sure?" she asked. "Only that?"

I nodded. Then again.

"All right," she said.

I hugged the book. I pranced to the smiling cashier and proudly gave it to her. Then we went home, and I read.

I read the fairy-tale book on Wednesday, lying on my bed after school. I read more of it on Thursday, lounging on the dining room floor. I read some of it on Shabbos, until Yitzy saw and said I wasn't allowed to; it was forbidden to read goyish books on the holy day. So I had to wait until Sunday, when I went to Blimi's house.

Blimi locked the door of her bedroom when I showed her the fairy tales. She stared at the cover, and then scornfully asked, "Why are you reading a book of the goyim? In my house we don't read books from the goyim."

I sat down, seething.

"It's not a *goyishe* book," I shot back. "It's a children's book."

But Blimi would not leave well enough alone, and wanted to know what the story was about, and why the princess was immodestly dressed. So I told her the tales of once upon a time, of magic, spells, and evil queens. I told her of princes and lovely princesses, and how they got married and lived happily ever after.

"'Cause that's the way things are in fairy lands," I explained. "There, people are allowed to fall in love."

But Blimi said it was all nonsense, things we shouldn't read. Because love isn't meant to be, not anywhere. Marriage is preordained in Heaven long before anyone is born or knows what love means. The only marriages meant to be are where the boy and girl meet with the parents' and rebbe's permission and then don't see each other again until their wedding night. Everything else is *shtism*, garbage.

"Hmph," I said, turning my back on her righteous face. "Then don't look."

But Blimi wanted to see. She peered past my hunched-over back, staring at the princess and the queen. I held my book protectively on my lap, blocking Blimi's view. She stood silently behind me as I read a fairy tale. Then, after a while, she sat down near me. She said that maybe she could read just one story. But only if I wouldn't tell her mother.

We lay on the floor and took turns reading a story. Then we read another, followed by another and one more after that. We read about Cinderella, Snow White, and the Sleeping Beauty. Then we had strawberry ice cream and it dripped all over Beauty and the Beast.

By then Blimi was giggling excitedly at the stories. She said she wanted to read "Beauty and the Beast" again. But we didn't have time, because her mother was calling us for dinner, and then I had to go home.

Before I went home, Blimi said I should bring the book to school. "Secretly," she whispered. "You have to! Then we can read it in the bathroom at lunchtime." She clapped her hands and then sighed. She said she wished she could be a princess, or at least have my book for the night. She'd hide it under her covers; her mother would never know. I promised that I would let her have it, but not today. But just for one night, and only if she promised to give me her snack for three days. Because she was my best friend.

Blimi gave me her snack on Monday, on Tuesday, and also on Wednesday. So on Thursday I tucked the book into my schoolbag, and we read "Sleeping Beauty" again in the bathroom during lunch. We sat on the windowsill by the toilet and took turns reading out loud. Not very loud. You could not bring just any book to school. It's not that there weren't any books written by goyim in our school library—there were. Books like Nancy Drew, Amelia Bedelia, and the Boxcar Children. But each book had to first be carefully read and approved by the librarian, and the bad words blacked out, before we were allowed to read them.

Fairy tales were not approved at all. If I was caught with my tales of love, the teacher would call the principal, the principal would call my mother, and my mother would call my father, who'd say that it's nothing, what's the big deal? Then my mother would come down to school to yell at me, or wait till I came home to yell even louder, and I'd be in a whole lot of trouble. It was complicated.

By the end of lunch, the prince had kissed the princess, and they'd rushed off to live happily ever after.

"*Yoish,*" Blimi said, sighing. "It's not fair. I wish I could be a princess."

"I know," I said. "Me too. Then we could live in a castle and have fairies for friends."

We sighed together. It was tragic, of course. Chassidish Jewish girls could never be princesses. Certainly not with goyish princes, and certainly not in those swirling immodest gowns that never covered the elbows.

Blimi shrugged. "Anyway, it doesn't matter," she said. "The stories aren't true."

"Of course they are," I said. "Just because they're *goyishe* doesn't mean they're not true."

Blimi snorted. "Fairies aren't real. And there's no such thing as magic."

I pointed at her triumphantly. "Yes, there is!" I said. "Moshe split the sea for the *yidden!*"

"That's not magic!" she protested. "That's a miracle."

"It's the same thing," I said. "A miracle is magic from Heaven."

Blimi looked at me. "Miracles can't happen to goyim."

I turned away in disgust. I was stumped. It was true. Such things happened only in our stories, true ones, filled with miracles that worked like magic, and prayers that worked like spells. Always, the Jews were rescued in the end.

Our stories were not like the tales of love. There were no goblins or ugly witches, no fairy godmothers with wands, no once upon a time or ever after. Our tales were holy. We did not need wizards, because we had rebbes. We had miracle makers, like Moses, the leader of Israel; Elijah, riding the chariot of fire; and the Baal Shem Tov, the founding rebbe of Chassidus.

The Baal Shem Tov was the greatest rebbe of our time. He knew the secrets of the heavens. He was a seer, an almost prophet who lived in the eighteenth century in Ukraine, a terrible time for the Jews of Europe. The Christians persecuted them endlessly with pogroms, expulsions, and blood libels, and their suffering was long and unbearable. Many Jews died or left the true way. Many despaired and said that God had abandoned them for another nation.

Then the Baal Shem Tov arrived, bringing hope to Jews everywhere. He was thirty-six years old when he revealed himself, a messenger from Heaven. The Baal Shem wandered from town to town, from village to village, wherever Jews were, healing the sick, giving to the poor, making miracles where they were needed.

The rebbe could make hunger disappear. When he traveled, time jumped at his command: a three-day journey turned into one. Mountains merged, valleys disappeared, so the Baal Shem could reach his destination faster. That way, if there was a Jew in a faraway town thrown into a dungeon by an evil bishop, the rebbe could get there in time for a miraculous rescue. Once, when some no-good gentiles threw rocks at a group of boys on their way to the house of study, the rebbe turned the rock throwers into stone. Another time, when soldiers with guns threatened him, he stared at them, and in terror they turned and ran, because beasts with guns are scared of true fire and holiness. The rebbe could see the future and talk with God.

After the Baal Shem Tov went to Heaven, his disciples— men like the rabbis of my mother's family—became the leaders, each community following its own rebbe. There, among the towns and shtetels of Europe, they told stories of the Baal Shem's doings, teaching joy and love for God. Often they became miracle makers too.

These were good stories, all of them important and all of them true. Still, there were no princesses in them. Only Jews.

The bell rang for the end of lunch, just as Rumpelstiltskin, in a glorious fit of rage, split himself in half. I jumped off the windowsill and grabbed the book from Blimi's lap, but she said she wanted to take it home. I had promised her that I'd let her, after three days of her giving me her snack.

"Um..." I said, pushing the book hurriedly into my bag. "Um...not today. Tomorrow, maybe."

"But you promised," she reminded me.

I had, but now I had changed my mind. I wanted to reread the entire book before I gave it away, even for one night.

Blimi stomped her foot. "You're a liar."

"I never said exactly when you could have it," I said. "And it's my book, so if you touch it, it's like you're stealing. It's a sin."

But Blimi said that lying was a much greater sin. "And anyway, my great-great-uncle was a big, important rabbi too, and he was more important and made bigger miracles than your ancestors ever did."

I said that everyone knew my great-great-grandfather was the biggest rebbe.

She said that everyone did *not* know, but she would agree if I'd lend her my fairy-tale book now.

"No," I said.

Blimi said I was a dumb friend. She said that I never shared snack with her, and she was never coming to my house again because I had a crazy, crazy, *crazy* brother.

I clutched my book bag and stuck out my chin.

"I don't care," I said. "I'm not your friend anymore, and I wouldn't let you come over anyway. And," I continued haughtily, "my great-great-grandfather will make a magical miracle from Heaven and my brother will be smarter than you. So there."

Blimi put her hands on her hips. "No, he won't," she announced. "He can't. Your family is cursed!" She smiled, looking satisfied. "That's why your mother and father moved to America after they got married."

I stepped closer to Blimi.

"My father moved to America so he could get rich! He bought the biggest house on the wrong side of the train tracks! He's almost a millionaire!"

"No, he did *not*," she said. "It's because of the curse."

"Huh?" I said. "If there was a secret curse in my family, I would've known about it before you!"

"Nuh-uh," she said. "Secrets don't work that way. Everyone knows except you—'cause you're a part of the curse."

She chewed loudly on her bubble gum.

"See?" she said, pointing accusingly at my book. "That's why your mother lets you buy things like *goyishe* fairy tales." Then, as I stared at her, thinking of what to say next, she slowly blew a gigantic pink bubble, crossing her eyes to see it.

I stuck my pinky finger in Blimi's face. Pop.

Sixteen

My father said that my mother was the most beautiful girl in Jerusalem. She had long, thick hair, red like fire.

He turned the page of their worn red wedding album. I squeezed next to him on the couch. On the yellowed pages, I saw pictures of my aunts and cousins with their hair piled high like beehives, wearing funny patterned dresses and clumsy pump shoes. And I saw my mother in a tiara made of silk flowers, her eyes glowing with joy. There, next to her, was my grandmother Miriam in a silk, rippling gown, while nearby a circle of women danced, holding hands. Across the partition on the men's side was a jumble of black hats. They crowded in front of the head table, where my father sat with my grandfather, my great-uncle, and the Holy Rebbe.

My mother looked like a princess. She and my father smiled happily at each other in the pictures, her necklace and diamond ring glittering. My father pointed at the photo. "I buy it myself," he said proudly. "Deh nicest jewelry your mother get."

"Where'd you have so much money from?"

"I vork hard," my father said. "I vork hard for a long time."

"But when?" I asked. "How old were you and Mommy when you got married?"

"We vasn't so young. I was tventy-four, your mother vas tventy-three."

I stared at my father in disbelief. "Twenty-three? *Twenty-three?*"

My father just smiled, turning the page. I shook my head.

There are rules, you see—always have been—that one must be married after eighteen and before twenty. By twenty-one, every matchmaker is involved. By twenty-two, special prayers are uttered at holy graves. And by twenty-three—by twenty-three . . . Well, there was no such thing as twenty-three. By twenty-three, you are married. You just are.

I pestered my father until he threw up his hands in mock despair. "Dat's what God vanted!" And he was off to shul for evening prayers.

I loved fairy tales because there was no such thing as breaking rules. The stepmother was always evil, the godmother was always kind, and the princess always slept for a hundred years without growing older by a day. She did not suddenly decide to sleep for only ten years because the curse was ninety years too long. And the prince, he always kissed the princess, no matter what. He never changed his mind, thinking that maybe he shouldn't kiss a half-dead girl he'd never seen before.

In real life, you could not give or take an extra month when it was time to marry. After nineteen, every year was like one hundred, and waiting too long messed things up entirely.

Blimi's cousin did not get engaged until she was twenty-one. This was not her fault. She had to wait for her diabetic older brother, who could not find a bride until he was twenty-two, after his mother forgot to lie to the matchmaker. Everyone said that Blimi's aunt had made a dreadful mistake, telling the truth about his diabetes. But it was too late, and in the end he had to marry a girl who had diabetes too. And though they had children who did not have diabetes, everyone said that they were lying about it and that they really all did.

But twenty-three?

Twenty-three?

I told my mother that I was to be married at exactly eighteen and not one second later.

"Of course you will be," she reassured me, twisting the kitchen knife in the keyhole of the bathroom door, which Nachum had locked from the inside. "Don't you worry. Of course you will be. Nachum—open the door!"

But I was very worried about getting married. My cousin Shaindel had told me that my siblings and I would be shunned in marriage because nobody wanted a family with a crazy boy like Nachum. I rolled my eyes but I knew she was right. Who would want to marry me when I turned eighteen, when nobody even wanted to come over to play?

Fraidy, queen of my class, refused even when I promised her my newest stickers from my sticker collection. Esty wouldn't come either, but she said it had nothing to do with my brother. It was because I lived in Flatbush. She wouldn't even call me on the phone. It was too expensive, she said, being long distance from Borough Park.

Only Blimi had come, and she had stared and stared at Nachum, and the next day had told Chaya Sarah and the others all about it.

Now, in spite of my impeccable rabbinical bloodlines, Nachum had ruined my marriage prospects. My mother said that I was being ridiculous. Marriage was *bashert,* preordained by Heaven. She said, "God plans, but man laughs." Or maybe she said it the other way around. Whatever. If it was meant to be, it would be.

But I knew that Nachum could un-*bashert* it all, because *shidduchim,* one's marriage prospects, were very important. In fact, *shidduchim* were so important that most families didn't even let God make things happen. No matter what God said, they simply wouldn't marry into a family that included Nachum.

It was like the time Chaya Sarah's oldest sister almost got engaged to a boy, but then didn't. Chaya Sarah had told me in secret that her sister would soon be a bride—her mother was so excited and it was all perfect, *bashert,* straight from Heaven. But at the last minute they found out the boy had had an operation on his head when he was six. He was healthy now—the family had medical reports to prove it—but still. It would have been *bashert,* but an operation like this was simply unacceptable. Who knew what was hiding in his head? My friend's mother was so hurt and insulted that she refused to speak to the matchmaker ever again.

There was a long list of rules about getting married, and there was nothing even God could do if one broke these rules. They were:

1. Don't wear the wrong color tights.
2. Don't wear denim.
3. Don't be too poor.
4. Don't be a *baal teshuvah* (a once secular person who repented and became religious).
5. Don't have a relative who is a *baal teshuvah*. (Tell him to stay secular.)
6. Don't have any medical conditions. If you do, lie to the matchmaker and say you don't.
7. Don't have a crazy child.
8. You can wear the wrong color tights, and sometimes even denim, if you have a lot of money.
9. You can be very poor if you have many dead rebbes or Torah scholars for ancestors.
10. You can have certain medical conditions if you have money *and* many dead rebbes or Torah scholars for ancestors.
11. Please. Don't have a crazy child.

This is why many families gave their crazy children away—so their other children could fulfill their destiny. Blimi's neighbor's parents had a Down syndrome child and had given him away when he was just born. So did the family who lived at the end of Blimi's cousin Nechy's block, but no one was supposed to know.

The rules made *shidduchim* easy for everyone to understand. It is the way everyone knows whom God wants us to marry, and whom He absolutely does not. But my mother didn't seem to care. Even for the sake of my future marriage, she wouldn't throw my brother away. I had once heard her say in an argument with someone on the phone that Nachum was a child, not a toy to discard. If God had given her this son, then He had meant for her to care for him.

She annoyed me, because she was using the *bashert* thing in all the wrong ways. If Nachum was *bashert*, meant to be, from God, then how come he made all our *shidduchim* un-*bashert*, not meant to be, from the same God?

I told Shaindel, irritably, that I could marry anyone I wanted, because Nachum was destiny sent from Heaven's throne. She said that it didn't matter where he was sent from because what Nachum had was genetic, and everyone knew this meant that all the grandchildren would be crazy like him. She also said that maybe Nachum was meant to be, but not nearly meant enough. The rules of *shidduchim* were still much more meant, and those were what would be.

I wanted to tell my mother that because she had selfishly not given Nachum away, I would never get married. I had no preordained partner in Heaven. I wanted to tell her that I wished she would be more like the other mothers, less tall and strong. I wanted to tell my mother this, but I did not.

Seventeen

Months had passed since my brother had come back from Israel—fall and half of the winter—and the very special Chush school had still not made him normal.

I began my forty-day fast.

The second fast was harder than the first one. By the third day, I realized it would be easier if I stayed home from school, away from Nechy's sour candies and Blimi's stupid cheese snacks. I could be hungry at home.

This should not have been a difficult matter. After all, it was my rightful turn to be sick. A few weeks before, I had made a deal with Miri after she stayed home from pre-1-A with a fever. I told her that I'd give her the pack of stickers I had stolen from Rivky if she would let me have a turn at being sick. She had had the fever three times already, and I hadn't gotten it even once. She said okay, grabbed the stickers, and stuck them all over the walls. But the next time came and there she was, taking my turn, burning up with

fever again. I told her that she was a liar, and it was my turn to stay home from school. She should get out of my mother's bed now.

Miri cried. She pushed me away and called my mother, who came quickly down the hall.

"What are you doing?" she demanded. "Why are you bothering her? And why are you still in pajamas?"

But before I went to my room to get dressed, I had the last word. I warned Miri that I would never make a deal with her again; that God sent liars like her straight to the fires of Gehenim for eternity and more. Also, she had better give me the stickers back like new, exactly the way they were when I stole them.

I went to school, finished snack and lunch, and said a prayer to absolve the food. I did this for the next three days. Two psalms absolved a sandwich, five a Super Snacks bag, eight for Milk Munch, and three for a piece of fruit I didn't even want.

Still, deals with sisters were easier than deals with God. It was clear when you were cheated and when you weren't. And when you were, you could pinch that sister, push her, stick out your tongue and make her cry. Then at least you felt better. With God, it wasn't so simple.

On the seventh night of the fast, I said fourteen psalms for eight Peanut Chews. Then I said my nightly prayers. I was just settling under my covers, chewing on gum my mother forbade in bed, when my father's voice exploded down the hall.

I had never heard my father sound like that. "You're wasting your time!" he shouted, as if he had forgotten that we were sleeping nearby. "You can't fix that kind of thing!"

My mother's voice rose. "Our child is not a waste of time!"

My father banged the table. "A waste! A waste! You're living in a dream!"

My mother responded sharply. My father argued back. Then there was a harsh sound: the squeal of the chair as it was shoved back, hitting the counter. I heard my father stride down the hallway. The front door slammed shut and he was gone.

I breathed deeply. I was furious.

My teacher said there were things we mortals couldn't understand. Only God knew. Only God saw. Only God could decide what was good and what was not, and it was our job to accept it with blind faith, because the ways of Heaven are mysterious and silent.

But I knew that this wasn't silence. This was ignoring. My family came from generations of great rebbes, so how could God just ignore them? And after I had not had Milk Munch for what seemed like forty days, after I had prayed devoutly every morning and night as I never had before—it just wasn't right. God had stolen my best prayers and had given nothing in return.

I moved the cover cautiously off my face. I looked over to Miri's bed, but her eyes were closed.

I tiptoed quietly down the hall. Nachum slept in the room right off the kitchen. He lay still, on his back, his eyes wide open, his left foot tied to the bed so he could not wander out of the house. I walked past his room and stopped by the kitchen, squinting in the light's glare. My mother was sitting at the table, but she did not see me. She was looking at the darkness of the window, her hands trembling on her lap, her face tense with silent fury, her eyes like two glimmering coals.

Eighteen

Once, in a little town in Poland, in the mountains of eastern Europe, a soul wandered, lost and alone. You see, when the soul had first departed from earth and had entered the heavenly court, God had examined it closely. The angels were silent. Would they accompany the spirit to the gates of paradise, or down to the searing fires of Gehenim?

Finally, from the heavenly throne came a verdict. The voice of God declared the soul not yet fit for paradise, but equally unfit for the fury of Gehenim. Instead, the soul was offered a third option. It must return to earth, where it would be born again to correct the sins of its past. If it succeeded, the gates of Heaven would open; if not, it would be sent off to the fires of Gehenim.

But the soul refused. It cried bitterly, lamenting its fate, and said it would rather go nowhere than be sent to earth again.

"So be it," thundered God. "Thou shalt go nowhere!"

And so the spirit was banished from the holy presence, fated to wander the ether, searching for final peace. One day, in its eternal exile, the lost spirit wandered through the cold, gray mountains of eastern Europe and to the outskirts of a small town. And it happened, by chance, that a young man was strolling there, alone in his thoughts and prayers.

The lost spirit was filled with joy, for it could see the purity that filled the young Jew's heart. This Jew's heart will purify me and lead me to Heaven, it thought. And with that the spirit plunged itself into the pious young man, who immediately collapsed in a dead faint.

A night passed. The time for morning prayers arrived. But the young man did not appear in synagogue. Immediately the town was alerted, for the boy, the son of the simple butcher Avremel, had never missed a prayer in his life, and certainly not seven days before his wedding to the daughter of Yossil, the town scribe.

Avremel, the simple butcher, followed by Yossil and the men of the town, searched everywhere in the surrounding forest, calling the young man's name. Hours later, they found him. Alas, he was mad, raving like a lunatic. Scrambling on the ground, he foamed at the mouth, muttering deliriously about things that weren't.

The townspeople picked up the poor groom and carried him back home. The simple butcher rushed to the rabbi in the house of study, with the worried scribe right behind him. It is a dibbuk! they cried. A spirit had leeched itself onto the boy, sucking out his very life!

The father begged the rabbi for a blessing, a cure. For what had the boy done to deserve this? And the wedding—the wedding! It was in seven days!

The rabbi withdrew into his corner room. From there he called for Moishel the Meshuganah.

Everyone in the shtetl knew Moishel the Meshuganah. He had wandered into the town one day some years back. Just passing by, he had said. Just passing by.

Moishel slept on a cot in the women's section in the synagogue, holding long conversations with himself. Moishel ate when the townspeople gave him food; when they didn't, he went hungry. But Moishel was really a hidden tzaddik, his brilliance disguised by a mask of insanity. Only the rabbi knew this, having seen him study Torah at night with Elijah the prophet himself. But, sworn to secrecy by Moishel, the rabbi kept silent. Now, though, he knew that only Moishel could help the afflicted groom.

The rabbi and the madman went to the groom's home. There they remained for three days, behind locked doors. Finally, on the third evening, the door opened. The townspeople gasped. For between the rabbi and the Meshuganah, the young man stood smiling shyly. Around his neck he wore an amulet.

In the amulet, the rabbi explained, were inscribed mystical words that had forced the unwanted spirit out of the groom's soul. The amulet must never be taken off, he warned. It must never be opened. As long as it remained on the young man's neck, the spirit could not reenter his body.

One week later, there was a joyous wedding celebration and the pious young man married the equally pious daughter of the town scribe. Together, they had many children who grew to be great saints unto the nation of Israel.

This is true. It says so in the Tales of Tzaddikim.

But all that happened long ago. Decades later, the young man—now an old grandfather—died, and the amulet disappeared, buried with him in the ground somewhere in Poland. Moishel the Meshuganah had commanded that it be so, lest the unwanted spirit reenter the man's body and obstruct his way to paradise. No one knew where the grave of the amulet was. Those who did held the secret until they, too, had passed on.

And this is why the rabbis of today don't have the amulet and no one can heal madness anymore. Not even my father.

Once, my father tried to cure Nachum's madness. Just once. After that, he did not try again.

It was the end of February, and nearly Purim, the last of the snow blanketing the streets of the neighborhood. I was nearly halfway through third grade. The twins from down the block were supposed to come for Shabbos lunch, but I was glad they did not, because between the first and second course, my father shook Nachum until he nearly broke.

My father and brothers had returned from shul promptly at twelve that Shabbos, and I could see from my father's face that it hadn't been good. Nachum had gone straight to his room, where he played with his Lego on the floor. My father came after him, sitting down near him to show him how to make a better bridge. But Nachum refused. He squinted anxiously. He rocked himself. He leaned protectively over the scattered Lego pieces.

My father left Nachum's room. He walked straight to the

dining room and poured wine into the kiddush cup. We all gathered around. My mother called Nachum but he wouldn't come. My father recited the kiddush blessing, and then, sitting at the head of the table, recited the blessing over bread and silently sliced the challah. My mother and Rivky brought in plates of fish. We ate quietly, dipping the pieces of challah into gefilte fish and mayonnaise.

Then Nachum walked in. He held a red Lego bridge in his hand. With the other hand he grabbed a slice of challah bread off the cutting board, stuffing some in his mouth. Then he turned away.

But my father caught him. He yanked the challah out of Nachum's hand and held him firmly by the arm.

"No," he said, pulling Nachum closer to him. "No." He held Nachum's chin between his thumb and fingers, turning my brother's body until they faced each other. "First, a blessing," my father said clearly. "First say a *bracha,* like this." And he enunciated the first word of the blessing slowly and loudly, waiting for my brother to repeat it.

Nachum did not.

My father pulled him closer.

Nachum twisted away.

My father gripped his hand, his arm around Nachum's waist. "One *bracha,*" he said very clearly. "Just one *bracha!* You can do it! Like everyone else! Say it after me, like this: *Bah-ruch!*"

But Nachum's eyes turned to glass. His body froze. He faced my father, but he could not see him, his eyes a dark blank, the look my father could not bear.

My father shook him so he should look, so the glass in Nachum's eyes should break. He held up the challah right by his pupils. "I will give you the entire challah if you say 'baruch,'" he said in a loud voice. "Just 'baruch'! Baruch! Look at my mouth! *Bah-ruch!*"

Nachum turned abruptly to the challah and, blinking hard, reached for it.

"No!"

My father grabbed his hand.

"No!"

He shook Nachum hard, like a rag doll, his face white with anger and frustration.

"Look at me!" he said in a terrible voice. "Say a *bracha!* Just one word of the blessing! Say it—please! Say anything!"

The veins on my father's forehead turned purple, and the back of his neck was a dark red. We sat frozen at the table, not daring to move. I looked at Nachum, writhing in my father's arms, ducking his head in terror. My father pushed back his chair. He shouted hoarsely.

"I will buy you a Lego, a flying horse! Just one word! I'll give it you! Say one word! *Baruch, baruch! Baruch, baruch!* Say 'baruch'! It means 'blessed'!"

Nachum's body trembled. It was as if he could hear thundering echoes, but not a single word. As if he could see walls crashing around him, but no faces. As if he was paralyzed, but could not run.

My father slammed the challah down hard on the table. The wooden cutting board flipped up, crashing onto the floor.

"Take it!" He pushed the challah into Nachum's hands.

"Take it, take it, take it. Eat the whole thing!" My father couldn't stop. It was as if he was ripping down the walls around my brother's mind with his bare hands, trying to tear my brother out of there, and drag him over to our side, where he belonged.

I looked across the table at my mother's empty chair, at Rivky bent over her plate, weeping softly. Yitzy, staring intently at his fish, sliced the gefilte into thinner and thinner pieces. Avrumi and Miri, their mouths open, stared at my father; they did not know who this man was.

My father shouted until his voice broke, until Nachum stood limp in his arms. The red bridge had fallen from his hand.

I got up from my chair and rushed into the kitchen. My mother was standing by the counter, her eyes pools of dark sorrow. Her hand gripped the fork, mashing, mashing the hard-boiled eggs.

"Make it stop," I told her, my fist rubbing away my tears.

My mother's hand moved steadily in the bowl. She pushed the fork in circles, around and down, around and down again. Eggshells were scattered on the counter. The saltshaker lay sideways near the sink. My mother sprinkled salt onto the eggs. Then the fork went around and down again.

I sobbed. "Why aren't you making it stop?"

The green blade of the knife moved swiftly up and down as my mother cubed an onion. She did not sigh. She did not speak.

"It will stop soon," she finally said. "Don't worry. It will stop."

It did. When my mother came into the dining room holding the egg salad, it had stopped. Nachum was no longer there. The challah, in pieces, lay on the floor. My father sat in his chair, hunched over the fish plate, in gravelike silence.

He did not sing the Shabbos songs. He did not ask my brother to say that week's Torah sermon. We ate the egg salad and then the meat, finishing the meal quickly. Afterward, my parents went to their room and we went outside to play in the cold.

Nineteen

It had been a bad day. Nachum had torn off large pieces of the wallpaper in my bedroom, the pattern of pink and violet swirls that my father had just put up. I had grabbed him and kicked him hard. I had scratched his face and pinched his arm, viciously twisting his skin. Nachum had shrieked, fighting back, and Rivky screamed at me to stop.

My mother had pulled me off my brother, but I kicked furiously in the air. I rushed at him again. I wanted to kill him, this time for real. But my mother dragged me back. Nachum ran down the hallway to his room as my mother turned the lock on my bedroom door, her enraged voice cutting through the hollow wood. "You don't leave this room for the rest of the day! You don't dare open this door!"

I sat on my knees on the floor. I gathered the shredded pieces of wallpaper in my hands, sobbing. I cried and cried. Then, still angry, I threw the pieces at the door, watching them fall to the ground. No one came down the hall to talk to me, or to whisper, not even Miri. I lay on the bed, breathing heavily.

It wasn't fair.

Wasn't fair, wasn't fair, wasn't fair.

I pulled books off the bookshelves, letting them crash onto the floor. I tore up Miri's pre-1-A drawing. I curled up on my covers, imagining my mother in the morning, her sorrow and regret when she found me motionless in bed, dead of misery and injustice.

Then I fell asleep.

When I woke up, it was dark. Miri was sleeping in her bed. The door to my room was open, but the hall lights were off. The entire house was still. It was strange being up alone so late.

I could see my fairy-tale book on the desk by the window, glowing faintly in the moonlight. I picked it up and climbed onto the desk. I read about the beast and the enchantress who had cursed him for his cold heart. I read about Belle, the beauty, and her poor father, Maurice, lost in the cold forest in search of a rose. Belle came to rescue him after he was caught by the cursed prince. The cursed prince then treated her very kindly and gave her beautiful clothes. But the townspeople came to kill the beast, not knowing that he was really a prince inside. Belle kissed the beast and he turned into a handsome man. In the end, Beauty and the prince got married happily ever after, because he repented his past evil actions, which, to the goyim, means falling in love with a beautiful girl.

The wind moaned against the windowpane. I pressed my nose to the glass, peering at the faraway stars. I could see my reflection in the window, hazel eyes, round face, one dimple. I wondered if I looked like Nachum. Blimi said I didn't, but still. Maybe I was really his twin, and they just weren't telling me.

I heard a sound from the kitchen.

I climbed off the desk, listening. I tiptoed out of my room and down the hall. A car passed by just then on the street, the flashing headlights lighting up the kitchen, showing a jumble of shadows. The fridge hummed, looming in the darkness like a dozing ghost.

I tiptoed past my brother's room, past my sleeping parents. In my mother's workroom at the end of the hall, the buttons on the fax machine blinked, curled sheets of waxy paper waiting in the tray. But what I saw first was the forbidden door. It had been left ajar.

I walked quietly toward the closet. The old bulb attached to the side wall shone faintly over the shelves. My mother had forgotten to shut it off. I looked down. The slat by the threshold where my toes rested stared up at me, beckoning.

I looked over my shoulder at the silent hallway. Then I bent down quickly, slid my fingers under the linoleum-covered panel, and pulled. The floor opened easily.

Underneath the false floor, in the deep and mysterious space, lay gift-wrapped boxes covered in silver, containers filled with old papers, and a red safe with no key. The papers in the containers were covered in small Hebrew writing. Maybe they were letters from the Holocaust. Maybe from the Inquisition. Chaya Sarah's father had letters from King Solomon when he built the first temple; he had bought them (she said) straight from a descendant of Solomon himself.

Near the gift boxes lay the wedding album that I had looked at with my father. Underneath it were other albums, an old green one and a larger beige one with faded words on the cover, both filled with pictures of my mother's childhood and marriage. Then I saw a small box tucked into the corner, behind the papers. Sitting comfortably on my knees, I reached over and pulled it out. I pressed it hard against my thigh and tugged at the cover, but it stubbornly stuck. I pulled and pulled, but still it would not come off. Then, finally, it did, and piles of pictures surged out, spilling onto my skirt and around my feet.

I sifted through the photos, mostly old ones in black and white, of tombstones and strange cities, of buildings and roads I did not know. Some of the pictures had people in them. Words and dates were scribbled on the back. I did not recognize the faces.

I took out the last batch of photos and stared. I could not understand.

In the first picture there stood a soldier holding a long rifle. He wore a khaki uniform, a helmet, and boots laced up over his ankles. The soldier pointed the rifle at the camera. There were more pictures of this soldier, pointing his gun proudly, or with his arms around friends, smiling. I saw an army truck parked behind him in one photo. In another, he was standing by the window of the driver's seat, looking intently ahead.

The last picture was half the size of the others, so much

smaller that I nearly skipped it. There a pretty girl with long hair stood close beside the soldier. She was laughing, and in her face there was joy. The soldier was laughing too. Both the girl and the soldier had sparks in their eyes, as if they shared a secret.

For a long time I sat by the closet, looking at this picture. I knew this soldier, with his badge and his khakis, his trimmed beard and his gun. Such guns they gave only to soldiers, men who fought in the army. I knew the girl too, with her long hair—red like fire, uncovered, unscarved—standing by the man as if it was nothing.

These faces I knew.

The girl with the red hair—that was my mother. And the soldier beside her, grinning, was my father.

Part III

Twenty

When my mother first walked through Aunt Tziporah's neighborhood sometime in ninth grade, she was shocked. She had never known that people could live this way, with families of eight in one-room apartments, with bathwater cooking in pots on the stove.

Tziporah's mother looked old. Her suffering was etched into the skin of her hands, into the wrinkles of her silent face. She did not wear makeup like Savtah Miriam; she did not have shoes that matched her skirts. When Esther walked toward Tziporah's apartment, she passed children carrying blocks of ice for the icebox, and barefoot toddlers with pebbles for toys. She passed old men on stoops waiting patiently for the Messiah, and women with glazed eyes, half mad from poverty, illness, and childbirth.

My mother had never known a fatherless girl before. She'd never been friends with a child who did not have both parents at home. She'd known of this side of the city, where the poor lived, but not like this, up close, where you could see the poverty strung up on sagging clotheslines, in patched pants and worn-out shirts, snaking through backyards and front porches.

Tziporah did not always come to school on Fridays. She stayed home to clean for the Sabbath while her mother and older sister worked. There were other such girls who missed school before the holiday, whose fathers had died years before, or whose mothers had long since gone crazy.

When Esther left home on Fridays, she asked the cleaning lady mopping the spacious, tiled roof porch of their home to notify her mother, out shopping for the Sabbath, that she'd be back soon.

The week before, Tziporah had paid an unexpected visit to my mother's family's apartment on Ben Kadosh Street. My mother had let her in, but first she had run down the hall to her father and frantically begged him to hide. He could stay in the master bedroom and write his papers there, she implored. Tziporah must not see that she had a father, one who was alive and well.

It was the same with parent-teacher meetings in school. Most of the students did not have a parent who could attend. Their older sisters came in their stead. For how many girls had a mother, both functional and sane, with the time and energy to show up, much less to come dressed in four-inch heels and a custom wig? Savtah Miriam did not like it, but my mother refused to let her go. Let Chana go instead, she insisted. It was embarrassing to be one of the only fortunate ones.

So my mother, walking to Tziporah's home, readied herself

for a quiet place, one filled with sadness and silence. She wondered what she'd say. The thought passed through her mind that maybe it was wrong of her to visit. Maybe Tziporah would be filled with shame.

When she arrived at Tziporah's building, she heard loud voices—laughter. A door to her left swung open. A group of teenage boys trooped out, chuckling, and she heard her friend's giggle from inside. Two children stood by the threshold, holding up a covered pan. Two more came up behind them.

Tziporah appeared in the doorway.

"Esther!" she shouted. "Come in! We were just talking about my brother's latest prank." She pointed to four girls who were laughing as they sat around the kitchen table cracking nuts and slicing up kiwis and apples.

It was hard to hear the sadness in a home that loud and happy, with neighbors coming by, friends strolling in, and the boys chasing one another in circles around the apartment. Tziporah didn't seem to know that she was a poor, fatherless girl. She did not seem to notice that she lived in a two-bedroom apartment with the only fridge on the block. The neighbors often brought food to store in the family's freezer: Koplowitz's chickens, Shteinmitz's kugels, and the widow Kleinbart's homemade ice cream. In the bedroom were a dozen thin mattresses piled high, six for the Eichenstein family, who had just emigrated from Czechoslovakia. No one seemed to think it strange that thirteen people had been sleeping in the hallway and living room of a two-bedroom apartment for the last three months. Friends and family strolled through the open door throughout the day, passing jokes, gossip, and fruit around the kitchen as if it was Purim. If there was misery, it got lost in the din.

"The house on Ben Kadosh Street was the center of society," my mother often said. "But the one near the border was the center of social life. Oh, the evenings we spent there, laughing..."

And Shloimy, Tziporah's oldest brother, was the funniest of them all. Everywhere he went, he was followed by friends. It was the Friday after that first one that my mother saw him. She heard an angry shout and a mischievous laugh. A tall boy—sixteen, maybe—rushed out the door, Tziporah right behind him. She was holding over his head a bucket of dirty water. The boy saw my mother. He flashed a wide smile, then leaped over the steps and fled.

"This is for my brother—for his head," Tziporah said. "For you!" she shouted at the receding figure. "Can't wait even a *minute* for the floor to dry!"

And that was how my mother first met my father.

Twenty-One

I told only Kathy that my father had been a soldier. She couldn't ruin my marriage. Nobody listened to gentiles. Then I told the twins down the block.

I didn't mean to say it. It was just that it had been in my head for so long, I didn't realize when it burst out through my mouth.

When I first told Ruchela and Leah that my father was a soldier, they didn't believe me. Then they did, and I wished they hadn't, but it was too late. They said it was almost like being a goy. Now we would really never get married.

I explained to Ruchela and Leah that I had been just joking. I had only *dreamt* that he had been a soldier. It was a very real dream. But they said that I was lying, and I was terrified that they'd tell their parents, who'd tell mine, who'd send me off to Israel instead of Nachum. So I changed the subject and told them about the swings that my father was going to build, right by the side of our house. Then Briendy, the twins' older sister, came by, hopped up the steps, and said, "'Kay, let's play school."

Briendy was horribly bossy. When we played school, she was always the teacher. If we didn't listen, she would hit us. I didn't want to play school now. I wanted to play only if I was teacher. Briendy hit me. I hit her back. She said I was committing a great big sin, because she was older, and in the Torah it said that I had to listen to her.

"Does not," I said loudly. "It says that I have to listen to my mother and father, and my mother and father never said you could always be the teacher."

Briendy said fine. I could be the substitute teacher, but only when she got sick. I said okay, I'd be the substitute teacher, but only if she got sick and died now.

She hit me again. I said, "You're the worst teacher and I'm the principal. You're fired!" Then Ruchela, Leah, and I ran away from her to the other side of our house. We hid behind a bush near the yard. We giggled and crouched down low. Ruchela was about to whisper something when I saw her eyes widen. Just then Briendy screamed *"Boo!"* right into my ear from behind, and I fell backward from fright. When I stumbled back up, Briendy was staring at something in the garden. I was going to tell her that she was the most evil person ever, and in the Torah it says all sorts of things about people like her, but Briendy wasn't listening. She was pointing at Nachum, standing near the bush at the corner of our garden.

"Look," she said.

Nachum was eating berries straight from the bush. They

were tiny berries, hard and dark, and Briendy said they were poisonous. We stared at Nachum eating them. He shook his head up and down as he ate, nodding to someone who wasn't there.

Ruchela and Leah turned to me. "He's eating poison," Leah said, her eyes opened wide.

"I know," I said. "But they're not really poisonous—my father, he said they're not really poisonous." I said this so it wouldn't look weird that I wasn't stopping him from dying.

My father had never said anything of the sort. The berries were probably poison; they definitely looked it. But I wouldn't have seen Nachum eating them if not for Briendy, so it wasn't my job to make him stop. Maybe this was God's mysterious way. He wouldn't make my brother uncrazy—that was too big of a miracle—but He could make him die from berries.

Nachum ate a lot of berries. He only stopped when a fire truck passed by. Then he went inside, his hands and face sticky and red. I followed him into the living room. I wanted to see if he would die. My mother came out of her workroom right then and cried out worriedly when she saw him.

"What is that?" she asked, holding up his hand. "What did you eat? What did you do? What in heaven's name is that?"

I didn't tell my mother what Nachum had eaten, because I wanted the poison to work. Nachum just shook his head this way and that and blinked his eyes, mumbling.

My mother washed off his hands. She wiped his face clean as he twisted away. Then I followed him to his room and watched him play, waiting.

Soon it was evening and we were all in bed. I stayed up,

still waiting. Nachum had fallen asleep already, earlier than on most nights, and I sat in my bed till close to midnight. I passed by his room to check and saw him lying very still, but I couldn't tell the difference between sleeping and dead and I didn't know how long it would take. Then I went back to my room and fell asleep myself.

When I woke up it was light in my room. The sun shone through the shades. A school bus honked outside in the street, and I heard my mother's admonishing voice: "Nachum, no! Not the cocoa! No!"

Nachum was sitting in the middle of the kitchen floor, his face smeared with dark powder. My mother had forgotten to tie his leg to the bed. He had spilled the entire container of cocoa out onto the floor while everyone was sleeping and was licking it off his hands.

He wasn't dying. He wasn't even sick. He was eating cocoa off the floor. The berries weren't poison, and Briendy was an evil, bossy liar.

Twenty-Two

In the end it was Yitzy who told me how it had happened between my mother and father. He didn't know the whole story,
but just enough. He told me all of what he knew because he
was bad with secrets. Also because I crashed into him holding
the picture of my father and his gun.

It was early March, and still gray and chilly, but inside it had
been a marvelous day. It was the end of Purim, my favorite
holiday, and I had dressed up as a Chinese lady. Nachum had
been dressed up as a cowboy who made weird faces.

Purim was a fun day, a celebration of the time centuries before when the gentiles in the Persian Empire had tried to kill
the Jews but failed. It was Queen Esther who had saved the
nation by persuading the Persian king to instead kill Haman,
the evil plotter who came up with the murderous plan. The
king allowed the Jews to hang the treacherous Haman and his
ten sons in the main city square. So it was an upside-down
day of joy and miracles, and the reason that, once a year, we

dressed up in merry costumes, and exchanged food, wine, and holiday money.

My mother had sent Nachum and me with a basket of strudel, pineapple, and wine down the block to the witch who lived in the corner house. The witch was a woman who my mother said was just an old, lonely lady, and who Briendy said was a witch, definitely a real witch—and as she was the one who lived in the house next door, I figured she knew better.

So I sent Nachum, basket in hand, to knock on the witch's door. Perhaps she'd turn him into a frog. He walked up the steps, basket and all, but then turned to me where I was half hiding behind a parked car. I banged furiously in the air to show Nachum how to knock, but he just laughed as though it was funny. He then stared at the doorknob for a long minute, and just when I thought I'd have to do it myself, he pushed the little black button doorbell.

The lady who was a witch opened her door. She peered at him, but she did not turn him into a frog. Instead, she took the basket and gave him twenty dollars. Then she closed the door, and Nachum came back down, looking at the money as if it was a mystery. I dragged Nachum back down the block, irritated at the stupid witch and wondering why, to-day of all days, she had to be nice. But then Nachum let me have the money in exchange for a perfectly round rock I found right there, so I forgave him for not turning into a frog.

*   *   *

It was late that night, after the festivities, that my mother told me I was to wake up early the next morning. Passover, she said, was in a little over a month, and the house was nowhere near done. The cleaning lady was arriving at seven sharp the next day to begin the great Passover cleaning with my room, particularly my mattress, which had a lot of crumbs because of all the snacks I ate there.

I was too tired to think of it until I lay in bed. Then I remembered the thing I'd hidden under that very mattress, the one that was to be cleaned first thing. It was a picture of my father as a soldier. It was the picture I'd taken with me from the secret place, so I could look at it sometimes before I went to sleep. The picture could not stay. By early morning my mattress would be pulled out, turned over, and tilted sideways against my closet doors, and anything found beneath it thrown out—or worse, put in the palm of my mother's hand.

I stood up. Gently I pushed up the corner of the mattress and pulled out the photo. I needed to return it to the secret drawer now.

I waited for silence, for the house to quiet down and the sounds of voices to fade. I nearly fell asleep standing, but the lights in the kitchen finally went dark, and the door to my parents' bedroom clicked shut. I counted to sixty and then ran down the hall toward the study, to my mother's closet. I wanted to put the picture back fast, maybe slip it in the space between the fake and real floor so nobody could see it and realize that it had been taken out. That's why I didn't see Yitzy coming from the other direction until I crashed right into his chest. I gasped and stumbled back. I watched the picture as it flew into the air, swirling once between us, then floating down and landing gently on the floor.

My hand reached for the photo, but it was too late. Yitzy had already seen it. He looked down at it, then at me. I looked up at Yitzy, then down at the photo. My father's gun pointed out from it. When I looked up again, my brother's eyes were wide and his lips formed a perfect O. We stared at the picture lying between our feet as if it had us under a deadly spell. We did not move. We did not dare bend down.

Then a mattress creaked. There were footsteps in my parents' room at the end of the hall. Paralyzed with fear, I stared at Yitzy and saw panic in his eyes too. He snatched the picture, grabbed my hand, and together we ran down the stairs.

It was five quick steps from the bottom of the staircase to Yitzy's room. He locked the door behind us for safety. We listened in silence to the movement above our heads. When it was finally still, we breathed.

Yitzy held out the picture.

"Where did you get this from?" he whispered, half angry, half wondering.

"From...from...from there," I stammered, pointing in a general upward direction.

"Huh?" Yitzy asked. "There?"

"Yes, there," I said. "There. In the room. Upstairs. In the drawer where Mommy put it."

My brother looked doubtfully at me.

"Mommy didn't put this in a drawer!"

And then, just like that, I could not hold it in any longer. I burst out in a defiant whisper. "It was in the secret place under the closet floor!"

Yitzy's expression changed. At first he looked plain surprised, as if he couldn't believe I'd go and do such a thing. Oh, he'd known about the place under the floor for a long time; it was no secret. But that I'd gone and rummaged through it? At night? By myself? I should've called him first.

But then he looked as though he was thinking, the way he did when he couldn't decide. I could see him wondering if he could trust me, could see the wavering in his eyes.

I sat very still.

In the end he told me what he knew because he was bad at secrets. He liked telling stories he wasn't supposed to tell. But he made me vow that I would not spill the beans to anyone else. A promise was not enough, he explained. A vow was what we needed, the strongest kind of promise, accepted as a pact not only on earth between men, but also in Heaven by God.

So I vowed that I would not tell, eyes closed, legs crossed, hands held out so he could see that my fingers weren't crossed. I agreed that if I ever broke the agreement, I'd lose half of my afterlife to Yitzy, as God Himself was witness. This was a very grave thing.

Yitzy didn't know the entire story, but enough of its parts and pieces, some from my aunt and some from his friend who knew from his older brother. The older brother had heard it from his father. Or maybe a cousin. Yitzy had put together bits of the story like scattered puzzle pieces, one here, another there, about the cursed-love thing and how it had come about.

Twenty-Three

Once, in the faraway land of Jerusalem, there lived three sisters who came from a noble family. The eldest daughter, Chana, was engaged a week from the day she turned eighteen, to a lucky young man from among the finest and wisest of scholars, and from a family of substantial means. And so it should have been with the second daughter, Zahava, more beautiful than the first, who became of marriageable age just twelve months after her older sister.

Zahava, the middle daughter, was known for her charm and intelligence, and her dark, lovely eyes, just like those of her mother, Madame Miriam Strauss. When Zahava walked down the street, Chassidim quickly bent their heads to the ground, so as not to stare at the slender, regal girl, dressed in fashionable yet modest clothes from the designer boutiques of Tel Aviv. A girl like that should have been contentedly married the way her older sister had been, but Madame Strauss was a very particular woman. She was particular about her diet, her clothes, her shoes, and the man her favorite daughter would marry. The phone in the apartment with the spacious roof porch rang shrilly day and night. Matchmakers arrived at the door unannounced. From far and wide, marriage prospects were suggested from the richest and most important Chassidic families of Israel, Europe, and New York.

The millionaire Glutnick promised a summer house in Switzerland. The Tybergs offered their eldest son, renowned for his brilliance and piety. Everyone wanted a bride like Zahava, with royal bloodlines, sterling character, and queenly looks.

But Zahava turned nineteen, and twenty, and then twenty-one, and still, for Madame Strauss, no man was good enough. If there was money, then he did not have the right looks; if he had the looks, then out there, there must be greater scholars. Menachem Strauss, the father of the noble sisters, tore out his hair in anguish and worry. His beautiful Zahava was nearly twenty-two.

"The greatest scholars have come and gone," he cried. "The princes in their prayer shawls have all married other, less choosy girls." And his queen and princess were still looking for a dream. It was not only his second daughter he was worried about, but the third and youngest, who sat waiting. Waiting and waiting. For tradition dictated that the elder must be married off before the younger, like the engine of a train whose wheels must start rolling before the second car can follow. There is simply no other way for a train to run.

Esther was quiet about how long her sister was taking to

make a match. But often, in the evenings, she'd leave her house. Sometimes she'd wait in the central bus station for the bus that drove across town. Sometimes, impatiently, she'd walk. She'd go out to where her central neighborhood ended and another began. It was there that she met with the soldier she loved; it was there that they could walk and talk for hours, far from peering eyes.

The streets were wider where they met, lined with wealthy residential homes and carefully tended rosebushes. Soon the soldier would finish his service in the army and would be free to build his life. He had joined for the family stipend and the free education, but now, three years later, his duty was nearly done, and Zahava was still not married.

In the secluded spots of the city's parks and on the streets where Jews who did not wear hats lived, the soldier and the youngest of the Strauss sisters pondered their lives and laughed, remembering the past. For they had known each other for years already, from when they were teenagers chatting in the kitchen of the soldier's home, when he was still only the oldest brother of Tziporah, her best friend.

No one but Tziporah and her older sister, Hadassah, knew of their secret love. They, of course, had known of it for a long time. It was Tziporah who had declared them to be a perfect match. But recently, she had followed the rest of her family and moved to New York, where there were jobs and opportunity, and where they did not have to be so poor.

Only the soldier had stayed, waiting, waiting for Zahava

to find the man lost in her noble dreams and for Esther to be free. But it wasn't just the waiting that was hard. It was not knowing what would come after. Because though Esther knew exactly whom she wanted to marry, she could not imagine how she'd get her family to agree.

Twenty-Four

The morning after Yitzy told me this story, I woke up early, because the cleaning lady had come at 7:01 to clean for Passover. I ate a bowl of cereal and napped on the couch, waiting for the yellow school van's strident honking. In the van, Leah had saved me a place, but I shrugged and walked past her because I wasn't in the mood. Instead, I went to the backseat, bumping all the way to school on the scratched-up bench as if everything was just regular, and nothing had happened.

But something had happened—something terrible. My mother and father had fallen into love.

I could not understand it. My father had lied to me. My mother had betrayed me. Without the Holy Rebbe's permission, they had just gone and fallen into love. Who in their right mind would do such a stupid thing? And now look at how much trouble it had brought upon us.

At first I was angry, but by the time we arrived at school,

that was gone. I felt only fear. I did not sing along during prayer time. I could not remember the right place in the holy book. I spent most of recess in the bathroom, and during English I gave my snack to Blimi because I wasn't hungry. Blimi told me that she'd let me copy from her homework, but I didn't really care. None of it mattered anymore, now that I was cursed. Because Nachum wasn't the only one named after my grandfather. I was named after him too. In fact, I had been named after him first.

My mother's father, Reb Menachem Baruch Strauss, had died a sudden death in 1978, a year and a half before I was born. My mother, consumed with grief, badly wanted to name a child after her beloved father, and waited for a son to be born. But instead, she gave birth to me, a girl. It was the *rav*, a Torah scholar certified to answer religious questions, who explained to her that she could use the female version of her father's name—Menuchah for Menachem, and Bracha for Baruch—until such time that a boy would be born. And so, on the Shabbos after I was brought home from the hospital, I was to be named after my grandfather: Menuchah Bracha Strauss.

But then my father changed his mind. He changed it on the way to the synagogue, two blocks before he arrived. Suddenly, half an hour before the naming ceremony that followed the Sabbath prayers, he remembered that no grandchild had been named after his own pious grandmother, the devout Bubba Tzirah, the one he and his brother Zev had jumped on as she lay dead in the bed.

My father thought it over for a moment, maybe two. Then he made his decision. It would be a compromise.

In the synagogue, he stood at the podium facing the Holy Ark, the tables against the walls filled with herring, kugel, and wine, as is traditional for these ceremonies, and declared my name to be Menuchah Tzirah Strauss, one half after my grandfather, and one half after my great-grandmother. "And may her father and mother be blessed to raise her in Torah and in marriage, and in good deeds. *Amen!*"

For days afterward, my mother did not speak to my father. Perhaps for weeks. But what she could not have known at the time was that it was not my father but an angel who'd put the thought into his head. It was God who'd made my father change his mind in that last, crucial moment, and then left him to face my mother, trying to explain.

It had been a miracle from Heaven, and it was the only reason I was sane.

I had been saved when my father changed his mind, but Nachum was doomed. It was he, a boy, who bore the full brunt of my grandfather's rage when he was properly named after him: Menachem Baruch Strauss. Because my mother's father, I knew, had never forgiven her for falling in love. It was said he died of a broken heart, and when she gave my brother his name, he cursed her from Heaven with a son who could not feel or love, who could not speak or understand, a child who would tear her sinful marriage to pieces.

I was certain that if I'd been named after my grandfather, I would have been crazy, just like Nachum.

When I came home from school, I went straight to my room, now spick-and-span and hopelessly clean for Passover. I sat in my blanket box with my diary, breathing in the scent of Windex and Soft Scrub as I tried to think.

I thought about my family. Were my mother and father meant to be or not? If not, did that mean that my entire family was never meant to have been either? And what was I supposed to do about that now that I already was?

If love cannot be, as everyone said, and my parents' marriage was not preordained, then had my siblings and I all come about by accident, an unexpected flaw in the Grand Master Plan? Could love be made forgivable, for example by repentance, or only through suffering as punishment? And once there had been suffering and punishment, did the marriage become okay, approved by the heavens after the fact? Perhaps God did change His mind, preordaining the unordained, unordaining the long ordained, switching and replacing the meant-to-be pieces of His vast, cosmic plan. It was impossible to know, which I thought was terribly unfair.

I thought about my grandfather and the half-a-name I carried. If love was not forgivable by suffering or repentance, then maybe even Bubba Tzirah's name wasn't enough to protect me. Maybe my grandfather still meant to curse me too. He was just waiting for the right time, when I grew older, and then suddenly he'd strike me with half the doom for the half-a-name I carried. Perhaps my grandfather was simply biding his time, waiting until the dawn of my bas mitzvah, or one week before my wedding night. Only then would he unleash his rage as I slept in my bed, and I'd wake up forever half crazy.

I could barely sleep that night, worrying that, in the morning, when my mother came into my room, I'd be mad like Nachum. Did it hurt to be crazy like that? Would I know that I was me? Would I be able to scream for help, to tell anyone that I was trapped inside the madness? I imagined opening my mouth and only funny sounds coming out. How would my father ever know that I was in there? How would my mother know that I was trying to reach her?

My cousin Shaindel said that craziness was catching. You could get it if you shared the same blood. That's why nobody wanted to marry me or my family. And maybe that's why it was enough for my grandfather to curse just Nachum. From there it would spread on its own, and I'd be infected by my brother until I was halfway gone.

I stood in front of my bedroom mirror, staring at my reflection. I looked closely into my eyes—would I know the crazy if it was there?—and then at the rest of my face, trying to imagine what the curse would look like if it came.

It was pitch-dark in the house by the time I fell asleep, murmuring the nightly prayers for the third time. Nightly prayers kept bad dreams at bay. Maybe they'd do the same for a curse.

Twenty-Five

The next day, Miss Smiley, the resource room teacher, called me out of class. She said that I was to start going to the resource room every day during math. Because I was dumb, she said, slow, crazy. Something like that.

All right, of course Miss Smiley never used the word "dumb." She said that I needed remedial help to improve my skills in math. But it meant the same thing—dumb, the beginning of broken—because the resource room was a place where stupid girls went, girls who did terribly in math or reading. It was embarrassing being pulled out of class by Miss Smiley, with all my classmates staring at me and knowing that I was going to the dumb girls' room.

It was all Nachum's fault, of course. It was in the blood. I'd gotten the worst of it not only because of our names but because I was closest to him in age, barely a year older. Why, we were almost twins. My teachers often said that I seemed to be in another world, spaced out completely. Sometimes I rocked myself to sleep, bumping my head on the mattress, back and forth.

My siblings did not share this danger. Rivky was smart and got As on her tests. Yitzy was a top student in yeshiva. Miri had taught herself how to read one fine summer day, and at age two Vrumi had the vocabulary of a four-year-old. Only I was going to the resource room with the stupids, because Nachum was just thirteen months younger than me and we shared the most blood.

Over the next few weeks, I vowed to stay as far from Nachum as possible. I pushed him down the hall if he came close to my room and ran away if he came near me. He'd given me enough of his crazy and I wasn't going to catch even one drop more.

Rivky got angry at me when she saw me doing this. She said that I was the most selfish and sinful girl she'd ever seen after I refused to stand near Nachum when we posed for a family picture.

It was a Sunday afternoon in April. My mother had laid out our holiday clothing especially for the occasion, and brushed my hair into an elegant half ponytail, just the way the high school girls wore theirs. Dressed up, hair combed, faces scrubbed to a shiny pink, we marched outside, where the photographer was waiting behind his black camera perched like a crow on top of the tripod.

But then my mother set us up in order on the corner steps of our house. She said, "Yitzy, stand here. Rivky, you there. Miri, come here—don't move from this spot," so that we stood in a V shape in order of age, with Rivky two steps behind me and Nachum just in front.

So I refused to pose for the picture. Not with Nachum only three steps down.

The photographer held the button he would click to take the picture.

"On the count of three," he announced. "Everyone say 'Cheese!'" I sat down on the steps, my arms folded over my chest, and said that I would not stand up until Nachum moved. He could pose near Yitzy, or Miri, or in the backyard. Just not near me.

My mother looked at me, exasperated.

"What does it matter where he stands?" she asked. "Just look at the camera and smile!"

But it mattered a lot, and for five long minutes I sulked. Finally, Rivky agreed to switch places, rolling her eyes at me all the while. Then the photographer said "One, two, three," and we all said cheese.

After it was done, Rivky called me a selfish brat whom God would shove into the deepest parts of Gehenim. So I was a selfish and sinful brat. At least I was a normal one. Being generous was useless if I was also half mad.

Three weeks after the family pictures, I stopped going to the resource room. I had scored a ninety-one on my math test, and Miss Smiley said that I no longer needed remedial help. I was up to my class level.

My mother proudly hung up the test on the fridge. My father said I was a genius, pure and simple. Mrs. Friedman gave me a pack of stickers and promised two colorful erasers if I did well again. She also told me that it just showed that I was smart, and if I'd only stop dreaming so much, I'd be among the best in the class.

I said thank you and that I'd try, but I didn't really care much, not about the stickers or the colorful erasers. Mrs. Friedman could keep them in her prize drawer or give them to someone else. I was just relieved, deeply so, that I wasn't crazy after all. The curse hadn't struck. Not just yet.

Twenty-Six

The Baal Shem Tov dressed up often as a pauper, wandering the roads and forests of western Ukraine disguised as a simple peasant. Few realized who he was. None dreamt that beneath the torn garments glowed a mystical soul.

Through the dark of night, the Baal Shem would study Torah. He bent over the pages of holy books in the synagogues of small towns and villages, while around him, all the world slept. On hard wooden benches, in the silence of the shul, the Baal Shem delved into the realms of Heaven until the sun rose. Then, with the first specks of light above, the Baal Shem would stand up. Holding a walking stick in one hand, a satchel in the other, he'd take leave of the small village to wander the mountains and forests once more, a vagabond, invisible to all.

For years the holy Baal Shem traveled in this way, until one day he reached the city of Brody. There he encountered a great scholar and rabbi who realized quickly that this was no simple man. Reaching out, the rabbi asked the unkempt wanderer many questions. When the Baal Shem realized that he could not hide from the persistent Jew, he stopped pretending and revealed himself. Together, the rabbi and the hidden saint engaged in many debates and discussions on the laws and ways of the Torah. Over time, the great rabbi grew so impressed with the Baal Shem's brilliance that he offered his daughter, Chana, for the wanderer to take as a bride.

The Baal Shem agreed, and the rabbi and the beggar saint wrote out a marriage agreement, one that remained just between them. For reasons unknown, they kept it a secret, and when the rabbi returned home, he did not tell even his daughter that she was engaged to a tzaddik in a pauper's disguise.

But shortly afterward, the great rabbi died, and the Baal Shem arrived at the family's home, with the marriage agreement in hand. When the son of the great rabbi, himself a renowned scholar, opened the door, he threw coins at the poor man and waved him off, eager to return to his studies. But the Baal Shem banged on the door again, shoving the paper into the son's hand as soon as it opened. When the scholar read the signed contract between the pauper and his father, he nearly fainted.

This uneducated boor? This man in torn clothes? There was no way his gentle sister from a noble family such as theirs could marry him.

"It must have been a mistake," he explained to his sister, Chana. "You don't have to do this...You mustn't."

But Chana insisted on marrying the beggar. She trusted her father completely, and realized that this man was destined to be her husband. Privately, the Baal Shem told Chana of his secret, but his bride told no one, not even her own brother. Appalled at the unbecoming match, Chana's brother convinced the couple to leave town and spare him the embarrassment, so the Baal Shem and his wife moved to a small hut in the Carpathian Mountains. There the saintly Chana dug lime and clay for a living, as the Besht (an abbreviation based on his initials) studied and meditated in the fields. This would be their home until the time came for the Besht to reveal himself to the world.

Seven years passed before that time came. Only at age thirty-six did the Baal Shem unveil his mystical soul to the world. It took several years more for the stories of his miracles to spread and his reputation to grow, but eventually that happened too. It was then that Chana's brother finally realized the truth. He embraced the Baal Shem as his rabbi and leader and became his most devout follower. At last he understood that it was his brother-in-law who had carried the noble blood all along.

And so it was.

The high school girl who babysat us before Passover told me this story. She also told me to hurry up. We needed to get to Mendelsohn's pizza shop quickly, before Nachum started acting up. It was only a few more blocks to Eighteenth Avenue. If I behaved myself, she said, she'd tell me two more stories on the way back home, but only if I did not fight with Nachum even once.

I promised no such thing.

Nachum should never have come with us to the pizza shop to begin with. He should have stayed home with my mother as he normally did, or gone out with the special therapist lady who cared for him sometimes. But things were different now because it was nearly Passover. With only two weeks left before the holiday, school was out, and the teachers, therapists, and helpers who normally kept my brother busy were cleaning and preparing their homes for Pesach. So my mother had asked a high school girl, Devorah, to take Nachum, Vrumi, and me for a few hours to the pizza shop in Borough Park, saying that it was out of the house with all of us, or she'd go mad.

Rivky and Yitzy had stayed home to help, and Miri was playing at a neighbor's house, so it was only my two younger brothers and me walking under the bridge to the other side, where the kosher shops were. I didn't mind the long walk. It was April and pretty outside. I saw white petals peeking out from little azalea bushes, and green leaves budding on the trees.

We walked past Mendel's pizza shop on Fiftieth Street. Outside the shop, I saw one of my friends from school leading her three younger brothers down the street to the park. In front of Shoe Palace on Forty-Eighth, I saw my teacher from second grade rushing to get into a livery cab while holding a pile of shoe boxes in her arms, a harried expression on her face. On the corner of Forty-Seventh, we wove Avrumi's stroller through a small crowd of high school girls walking in and out of Designer's Paradise, holding bags of holiday clothes. Then we passed Landau's Supermarket, and the beggar man sitting on his plastic crate, angrily shaking a cup in the faces of passersby and proclaiming, "*Tzedakah, tzedakah,* buy your place in paradise!," and spitting at those who would not. Mendelsohn's pizza shop was on the next block, a narrow, crowded space bursting with families of six to twelve, all out before the holiday.

Nachum, who had been calm until then, turned agitated when we went inside, but Devorah, squeezing Vrumi's carriage through the aisle, never noticed. When we reached an empty table by the back wall of the pizzeria, she sat Vrumi down on a plastic baby seat and shoved the folded-up stroller under the table. She pointed a finger at me.

"Don't move," she said. "Stay right here on the bench. I'm going to get the pizza. Make sure Nachum doesn't go anywhere until I come back." Then she turned and walked across the store.

I could see the line for pizza stretching from the counter to the restroom at the other end of the shop. It was hard to hear anything over the men shouting orders, and the older sisters hushing younger ones, and the babies babbling from every corner. Nachum, sitting close to me, kept his head down, and I could hear him saying "Hungry...Hungry..." to himself. I told Nachum that I was hungry too, but that we'd eat very soon. The babysitter was waiting in the long pizza line. She'd bring fresh, hot pizza in just a few minutes.

But Nachum was hungry. He was hungry right now. And it didn't help to tell him to stay in his seat, because he didn't understand how to listen or wait.

Nachum stood up, his eyes shifting, his jaws moving as he bit his tongue. He blinked urgently as he looked around. Then he stopped, his eyes on a lady dressed in fancy white clothes and perched on a plastic chair at a table right in the middle of the shop.

The lady did not see Nachum coming. She was talking to the four girls who were sitting around the table, wearing matching pink sweaters and skirts. In her left hand, she held a wet napkin and pointed to a stain on one of the very pink sweaters. In the other hand, she held a slice of pizza, folded and wrapped in a large paper towel. The girl took the wet napkin from her mother and dabbed worriedly at the stain. The lady shook her head, her black wig shining, and then lifted the steaming pizza slice to her mouth.

But Nachum grabbed the slice of pizza right out of the lady's hand and shoved it into his own mouth, chomping down on the melted cheese.

The lady gasped. She stared at her empty hand, and then at my brother, gripping the pizza, tomato sauce dripping from the sides of his chin. But Nachum never looked at the lady—only at the pizza. Then he turned with the slice and walked back down the aisle toward our table.

I slid to the end of the bench as fast as I could. I slumped low, trying to sink into the ground, where no one could see me. The lady was now coming after Nachum, her eyes slits of outrage and disbelief, but following at a careful distance, until he reached his seat. She looked around, searching for a mother.

Then she saw me. Her eyes bored into mine. She asked me where my mother was, and I pointed to the long line.

"Babysitter," I whispered from where I was slouched at the farthest corner of the table. The lady stared at me as if I knew the secret of Nachum and why he had grabbed her slice of pizza. I looked back at her, saying nothing, because I really did not.

The dressed-up lady finally turned. She sat back down at her table with the four girls in matching pink, who whispered to one another and stared. She kept looking back at us, waiting for the babysitter to come.

But Devorah was still waiting in line, and now Nachum wanted ice cream. I knew he wanted ice cream, because I had been getting a snack for Avrumi from the folded-up stroller, and when I looked back up from under the table, I found Nachum holding a cup of someone else's dessert.

My brother stuck his finger in the ice cream and licked. I cringed, looking fearfully around, but nobody seemed to notice or care. Maybe he had taken it out of the garbage, I thought. Maybe someone had given it to him. I looked to the middle of the store, but the lady in white was busy cutting up another slice of pizza.

So I licked at the stolen ice cream along with Nachum. He didn't mind, and even held out the cup for me to share. And when we couldn't reach the bottom half of the cup because there was no spoon, Nachum simply turned the whole thing upside down, shaking the ice cream out onto the Formica tabletop.

The ice cream was good, even on the table. Nachum slurped some, and then waited for me to do the same. He giggled watching me, my face covered in white, licking off the tabletop with nothing but my tongue. I laughed when it was his turn too. Then we both giggled, because it really was funny, slurping up the ice cream, one after the other, always just in time to catch the melting ooze right before it slid to the floor.

Just then the babysitter returned from the pizza line. She towered above us, holding up a steaming pie. As she stared down at our sticky faces, behind her the lady in white looked ready to get up and come over to us. From another table we heard a boy exclaim, "My ice cream! A *ganuv* took my ice cream! Where's my ice cream?" Devorah set down the pie with a thump, her eyebrows high up on her forehead.

Grabbing a few napkins, she swiped at Nachum's cheeks. Then she ordered me to the bathroom sink, saying she could not believe what we had done. But Nachum wanted the ice cream from the table, the ice cream that she had wiped up. He stared anxiously at the crumpled napkins in the babysitter's hands.

"Ishe cream," he said loudly. "Ishe cream!"

"No," said Devorah. "There is no ice cream. Not for any of you. Pizza will be enough."

Nachum leaned forward, straining his neck.

"Ishe cream!" he said louder, his eyes clenched shut. "Ishe cream. Ishe cream. Ishe cream—"

"You already had ice cream," said the babysitter sternly, dropping the napkins into the trash. "No more." But Nachum lunged forward abruptly, his head crashing into the table, because he could see ice cream, both chocolate and vanilla, in cups and cones everywhere. He could see ice cream in sticky hands and on cluttered tables like a bright white light in a blur of movement and faces.

Nachum rocked hard. He screamed, "Ishe cream! Ishe cream! Ishe cream! Ishe cream!" His voice spiraled up into a high-pitched frantic shriek and bounced off the walls of the shop.

The lady in white behind the babysitter froze. A large family tumbling in through the shop's entrance stopped cold. Nachum rocked back and forth, faster, more furious, until his skull hit the table with that sickening thud. He was still chanting, *"Ishe cream, ishe cream, ishe cream, ishe cream, ishe cream, ishe cream!"*

The lady of the stolen pizza slice stared at him, her brightly painted lips hanging open. A waiter on the way to a table halted, balancing his tray of food in midair. Everyone in the shop was looking at us. Girls with high ponytails and boys with gelled side curls edged closer to our table to see.

A kind man with a beard walked hastily toward us. He looked worriedly at Nachum, maybe wanting to help. But then he stopped short, the loud whispers of his wife pulling him back.

Devorah leaned over Nachum, trying to stop the screaming. She whispered frantically into my brother's ear, but Nachum never heard her. I could see tears welling up in her eyes as she turned and rushed to the front counter, ignoring the long line. The man holding the ice cream scoop looked at her, at first bewildered. Then my brother's high shriek cut through the store again, and, startled, the man jumped and began shoveling ice cream hurriedly into a large cup. The babysitter grabbed the cup right out of his hand and ran back to us.

When she reached our table, she stopped. Then, gripping the cup like a weapon, she aimed straight for Nachum's mouth, holding the ice cream inches below his chin just as it came back down. There was a soft thud, as my brother slammed his face right into the cup. He gasped at the cold shock, jerking his head in surprise, blobs of ice cream like puffs of little clouds all over his chin and mouth. But Nachum stopped screaming.

There was silence in the store. I could hear the rhythmic whirring of the fan blades above. The babysitter was still holding the ice cream, but now she handed it to him and he clasped the cup as if it were a lost treasure. There were mothers and fathers, uncles and aunts, sisters and brothers in Mendelsohn's pizza shop, and they all watched as the babysitter grabbed Vrumi, the stroller, our bags, and our jackets as fast as her hands could move. They watched as she gingerly wrapped a hand around my brother's arm. They watched as she moved him cautiously forward toward the door of the shop.

I followed right behind. We walked down the aisle, through the crowd of gapers and starers as they cleared a wide path, careful not to touch my brother and catch whatever it was he had. The kind-looking man with the beard opened the door, following us with his eyes until we crossed the avenue and he could not see us anymore.

I sobbed all the way home. I hadn't gotten pizza or ice cream. But Devorah rushed ahead, telling me only to hurry up. My mother would give me whatever I wanted when I got back home.

Nachum was quiet now. He stayed calm even as the babysitter dragged him by his sleeve, pulling him along until we reached Avenue I. He held the ice cream cup high up, tipping it over his mouth, gulping globs of ice-cold chunks as if they were juice, until there was nothing left.

When we reached our block, I ran from the babysitter and into our house, into my blanket box. I could hear her coming up the stairs now, nudging Nachum and Vrumi inside. Faintly, I could hear her speaking to my mother, trying to explain what had happened.

I don't know how much she explained or how much my mother understood because I stayed crying in the box, planning vengeance on my brother and God. A few minutes passed, and the babysitter left. I could hear her heels clattering down the steps and carrying her out the red gate, never to be seen again.

Later that evening, I told Rivky that Nachum should be sent back to Israel immediately. Everyone would be happier that way.

Rivky said I was mean. "He's my brother," she said. "I want him to stay with us."

I grimaced. "No, you don't," I said.

My sister looked at me, trying to sound disgusted. "Yes, I do."

Now I was mad. "You're lying," I shot back. "You're just

saying that, but you don't mean it even a little." And I reminded Rivky of last year, when Nachum had been in Israel from June to September and she hadn't missed him at all. She hadn't said his name even once. Nobody did.

But Rivky said she had missed our brother, secretly, deep inside her heart. "I just didn't say it out loud." Then she walked righteously away.

I stomped my foot. Goody-two-shoes liar! She had not! Nobody missed Nachum, inside or outside their heart.

Twenty-Seven

There was the Holy Rebbe and, to his right, his brother, the one who'd be rebbe after him. There was my other great-uncle, the youngest of the rabbinical brothers, and at his side my grandfather, shaking a well-wisher's hand. In between them sat my father, with his trimmed beard and round, fur *shtreimel,* a soldier in a Chassid's land.

In front of the head table on the wooden dais where they sat, crowds of Chassidim thronged. They pushed forward, struggling to touch the rebbe, black hats bobbing up and down like a dark, churning sea.

I pored over the pictures in my mother's wedding album for hours. My mother had agreed to take it out to keep me busy, and I sat on the couch all evening, studying it, wondering at the questions I'd never ask.

There, under the plastic sheath, was my grandmother Miriam in a long, rippling silver and mint-green gown. Next to her, Zahava and Chana smiled prettily for the cameraman.

In another photo, under a velvet canopy stood a sage uncle reciting a blessing over a cup of wine. Near him swayed my grandfather and my father, their eyes closed in prayer, thin, braided sashes tied loosely over their long, dark coats. Toward the front sat the women, far from the men, wiping away tears and murmuring prayers.

I had looked at the wedding pictures in daylight, in lamplight, and in the moonlight to find my grandfather's curse. Curses were wrathful things, wounded and enraged, usually hidden beneath stiff, angry faces. But it was hard to know a story from a picture, to know what really happened just by looking at eternally frozen smiles. The problem was, I knew that angry fights and dark secrets never revealed themselves for the camera, never showed up in the darkroom. But somewhere behind the expressions in the photos was the broken spirit of my mother's father, watching and waiting, unforgiving of his youngest daughter's betrayal.

Yitzy had told me that night in his room, along with the other bits of the story, what my great-aunt Frieda had told him one day when she forgot that he was only ten at the time. She had said that the morning after Zahava's engagement, to a perfect young scholar from a city nearby, the matchmakers had come for Esther. Why waste even one more day? they said. There weren't many possible husbands left for a girl way past marriageable age. Did it really matter if they suggested a list of distinguished names a week before or after her sister's wedding?

They approached my grandfather in the synagogue and my grandmother in the bakery or in the street. Esther might be old, but no matter: she was still beautiful, and the family heritage would make up for her being twenty-three.

But Esther refused to hear the matchmakers. Not until after Zahava's wedding, she said.

Zahava's wedding came just a few months later, and then it was done. On the other side of the city, where my mother and the soldier walked, they knew they could not wait for even one more Sabbath to pass. Esther had to tell her father, her mother, and her beloved Bubba Miril now, that very day, that a matchmaker would not be necessary. She already had her groom.

Exactly how and when my mother told them about the man she was to marry, Yitzy could not say. Not even my great-aunt Frieda knew exactly what had gone on in the apartment on Ben Kadosh Street. Only that when the conversation ended, the heavens above the ancient city seemed to darken, and all hell broke loose.

Within hours, the rebbe was told and the uncles found out. Within a day, Savtah Miriam was standing on the roof, her screams echoing over the neighbors' yards. She screamed about their honor, their long, dynastic pride, and about her suffering in the Holocaust: *"Is this why I survived?"*

By Friday evening, the scandal had rippled and spread through the neighborhoods on both sides of the city. It made its rounds among the synagogues and the men walking down Geulah Street. It made its way through crooked lanes and opened shutters overlooking courtyards, through groups of young mothers watching their children play and passing around half-baked truths about Esther and her soldier groom.

The scandal circled the *shtieblich* where young men met to gossip and pray. It reached the porches where elderly women sat above the chatter of passing girls. It made its rounds, and then made them again, until everyone had offered their thing or two to say about a girl who prances about until way past marriageable age.

And such a fine girl. Who would have thought?

It was good, some said, that Esther's Knesset minister grand-father had died some years before. His bones must be turning over in his grave beneath the ground of the sacred Mount of Olives. Because a Chassidic girl does not find her own husband. A descendant of great rebbes does not marry a man she actually knows. And if it wasn't bad enough that the man had been a sol-dier, to make things worse, he was also a fatherless boy.

A pious girl does not sign her own agreements. A descend-ant does not, ever, marry a fatherless waif. Pity him, maybe give charity—but marriage? No matchmaker would suggest such an insult. Even the simple girl with no more wealth than an intact family did not marry a man bereft of a proper parent.

Why? Because. Some questions don't need answers.

Why? Because. And that's what mattered: tradition, hier-archy, and the way of doing things, the way it always was and had always been.

In a room closed off to all, Esther sobbed to Bubba Miril for days, begging her to understand, to meet the boy—to speak with him, at least. She could not bear to break her father's heart, but she simply would not marry another man.

This went on for weeks. Well, not weeks, but certainly many days. Or months. Yitzy wasn't sure.

"And then," he said. "And then..."

He was quiet.

"Yes? What happened then?" I asked. But he didn't know.

"Did they run away?" I helpfully suggested, but he could not say. Because it was just about there in the story that my great-aunt Frieda remembered that Yitzy was only ten years old, gave him some chocolate, and sent him off to play. So he never heard the rest of the story: who convinced Bubba Miril and my grandfather and who, if anyone, got my screaming grandmother off the tiled roof porch.

"They didn't run away," Yitzy said. "They got married. Even the rebbe was there." But he wasn't sure how. A year or so later, there was definitely a wedding—we had the pictures to prove it. But Yitzy said that it must have been a terrible time, full of blame and whispering. He knew. He'd even seen a rebbe point at Nachum roaming the halls in cheder, and heard him tell another, "See? Good things don't come from such a marriage."

I asked Yitzy whether our parents realized that they were cursed, but Yitzy shook his head fearfully and said that he had no idea. This was not the kind of question one asked a mother or a father.

It was nearly ten when my mother found me sitting on the living room couch with the wedding album. I had shifted my legs and was stomping and kicking at the air, trying to wake up my tingling feet.

"Your bedtime was at nine," she exclaimed. "Who are you kicking? Well, what do you expect? Sitting for hours..."

She took the album out of my hands and put it away. I listened to her walk down the hall, heard her in her even tone repeatedly tell Nachum to go back to bed. Slowly, I shuffled, half hopping, to my room. Miri was already asleep.

I sat on the desk by the window.

In the fragments I had gathered from Yitzy, it was hard to know the scandal from the truth. Had my great-great-uncle the rebbe blessed the marriage as an emissary of God, or simply as an uncle, only on his own behalf? Maybe my grandfather could not bear his daughter's tears and had appealed to his uncle for help. Perhaps it was Bubba Miril who could not watch my mother's pining and sorrow and who pleaded with her brother, the Holy Rebbe, to have a word with the heavens, to bless the girl already, despite the Grand Master Plan.

But one cannot force God's hand. One cannot change the divine will with emotions or sheer desire. You could say you spoke for God, but you could not change what it was He wanted to say. Such things could only end badly, even for saints.

I sighed and watched Miri sleeping, an open book over her snoring face.

It was hard to know the scandal from the truth, but one thing was certain. The blessing given by my great-great-uncle could not have been genuine, or there would never have come such a curse.

Twenty-Eight

Mrs. Friedman told me that she knew things were hard at home. She said she knew it was frustrating living with a brother like that, but that one day things would get better.

"God gives us only what we have strength to receive," she said kindly, as I sat at my desk alone. "Your mother is a strong and powerful woman, like her father and grandfathers." Then she told me about a renowned scholar who stood up in respect every time a crazy person walked into the room. "He said they were higher souls."

I stared glumly at Mrs. Friedman. It was recess, and my friends were running wildly outside. But Mrs. Friedman wasn't finished with my brother.

"The saintly scholar explained that all such souls had once belonged to tzaddikim who had been returned to earth by God to rectify a sin from their past lives. Children like your brother have a holy mission, to serve as penance, however tiny the flaw, so the holy soul can achieve divine perfection. That way, when they go back to Heaven, their perfect, glowing soul is sent straight to the highest level of paradise."

Mrs. Friedman also explained that God did not drop such a spirit just anyplace when He sent it back down to earth. He searched long and hard for the right mother and the perfect family who could take care of this very high soul.

Mrs. Friedman said that everything was for the best and that one day, when I grew up, I'd understand. Until then, if I'd only try to look differently at my brother, I'd find the good in what seemed only bad.

But Mrs. Friedman did not know what she was saying. She did not know that my brother wasn't a higher soul, only a broken one. She did not know of the tap, tapping angel, striking my brother's lip just a tad too hard until his mind was completely gone.

Then again, Mrs. Friedman did not have a crazy brother. She didn't have friends whispering behind her back. So all day I stayed just as glum as when she'd spoken to me, until something happened that made me rethink all that I believed.

It was that very evening when, by accident, I found a very good thing.

I hadn't been trying at all. I didn't care about finding the good side of my brother's special mission to atone for some past saint's life. Instead, I fought with Rivky over her new markers and then marched angrily to the living room to mope.

It was there that I saw it, the gift box I'd been eyeing for two days, the one my mother had received from her close friend. My mother had warned me to keep my little hands off—"Don't even think about it!"—but I desperately needed to know what was inside. And the package just *lay* there, alone on the shiny glass dining room table, white wrapping sticking out of the half-opened lid.

Looking around to make sure no one was there, I reached for it. If I did it fast, my mother would never know. The problem, though, was the gift itself, wedged tightly into the Styrofoam. I had to pull really hard until it finally came right out, too hard, too fast, and straight onto the floor.

I winced and stared down at the porcelain fragments of my mother's dear friend's gift. I listened for quick footsteps, for a shout, but there was silence. I had only seconds to run.

I rushed to my room. Once there, I grabbed a book and lay on my stomach on the bed, as if I'd been doing nothing but reading all along. Ten minutes later, my mother came in. I was up to chapter four.

She was furious.

"Did you break the porcelain plate I just received?" she fumed. "Were you the one who took it out of the box when I specifically said not to?"

I shook my head vigorously.

"No," I said. "It wasn't me. It wasn't! It was Nachum, I think. I'm almost sure! I saw him standing in the dining room before, right by the table."

The anger etched into my mother's face instantly disappeared. Her eyes, which had flashed with fury, now just looked tired. She shook her head slowly. Then she walked back down the hall without another word. This was a very good thing.

Somewhere inside my heart, I felt a little bad, but in the rest of my body, I knew it was all right. Because it struck me with clarity that this was the good I was to find if I only looked differently at my brother. It was like that when you had a crazy sibling. You could blame him for stuff he'd never done, because Nachum never got punished, no matter what. At most he'd get a gentle scolding from my mother.

So there it was. I'd been blind to the good that God had placed right in front of my eyes, but now that it was clear, I felt a renewed wonder for the mysteries of the divine plan. And I started to blame Nachum for everything.

I blamed him for the Super Snacks I'd eaten, and for Rivky's missing markers hidden in my drawer. I blamed him for the mess in the bathroom, and for the strawberries and sugar splattered on the floor. I blamed him for other things too, and these were also all part of the divinely placed good that I had found. It could have gone forever this way, if only my heart hadn't betrayed my happy thoughts.

But that feeling somewhere in my heart unexpectedly grew on the second or third day. It began when I blamed Nachum for the third time, and he blinked, bewildered, at my accusing finger. The feeling grew heavier by the fifth time; by the sixth, it was weighing me down as I walked around. But it was at night after prayer when it was the worst, pressing down on me so I couldn't breathe, and could barely sleep.

It was as if a boulder had settled itself right in the center of my chest. In my entire life, I had never felt as uncomfortable inside my own self. It made me irritable, and angrier than ever at Nachum. You'd think with the trouble he'd made, and the damage he'd done, he could take the blame for a Super Snacks or two, but no, of course not. Not with that dead saint inside. Not with that nearly perfect inner glow. Nachum and his stupid, high soul.

So the next morning, I repented. I asked Nachum to forgive me, please, so the terrible feeling should go away. This wasn't simple, because I first had to convince my brother that I was there at all.

I sat right near Nachum on his bed as my mother made sandwiches in the kitchen. Though I sat inches from him, he seemed very far, somewhere on the other side of his mind wall. I spoke quietly, my voice just above a whisper, because my brother was playing with his socks, and it felt silly apologizing to someone who couldn't hear.

But I said that I was sorry anyway. I told Nachum that he needed to forgive me, he had to, that if he didn't I'd make him miserable for the next three weeks. I confessed about the porcelain plate, the Super Snacks I had eaten, and promised never to do those things again. I spoke clearly, leaning toward him as he fidgeted and watched my lips move as if trying to decode the strange babble of a foreign language.

But then Nachum lost interest and stood up to wander off, and I was forced to pull him back down by his wrist. Because, really, if he was to rectify any of the past errors of an imperfect soul, he simply had to learn to stay in one place long enough to forgive.

I asked him again to accept my apology, but still, he didn't hear, and as soon as I let go, he got up, trying to leave again. I followed him, blocking his way to the door. I repeated myself urgently, because, again, I had no choice—I needed to be done with the apology before the yellow van arrived to take me to school.

"Do you forgive me?" I asked Nachum. "Do you? Yes? Nachum, yes? Say yes, Nachum. Say yes. Like this: 'Yes, yes...'" And finally, Nachum nodded. He said, "Yes, yes," as if mimicking a song. Then the van honked outside, and I ran out.

I sat next to Leah as she chattered on and on. In my chest, my heart danced, light as a feather. I had left my school-bag behind the door, and my lunch on Nachum's bed, but the boulder was gone; I could breathe again. I was purified, cleansed of all sin.

Twenty-Nine

Still, I told no one about the good I had found and then lost, deciding to keep it to myself. Because in the end it didn't matter what kind of soul my brother had. My father refused to keep him any longer. He said it was Nachum or it was the family.

Nachum wasn't better; he was worse. He did not speak, not even a sentence. In the dentist's office, he left teeth marks on the dentist's hand, and they had to tie him to the chair with a rope. In school, the teachers said he was a hopeless case after he made a hole in the classroom wall, crashing his head so hard against it that the Sheetrock caved in and broke. In the foam wading pool in our backyard one hot afternoon, he took off all his clothes, and then he walked down the street naked. And in the shul yard on the Sabbath, my friend's mother did not let him walk near her daughter, shooing him away like a stray cat.

"Away, away!" she had ordered, waving her hand frantically at him. "Shoo! Shoo! You can't come here! Away now!"

The boys in shul chased after Nachum every week, chant-ing, "Crazy boy! Crazy boy! *Meshuganah!* Crazy boy!," and Nachum would run from them this way and that, blinking and flapping his arms like a frightened pigeon.

Sometimes I prayed that my brother would get sick. Then the community would pity us and feel kindly toward our plight. Our friends and family would gather closely around to advise and pray and help. Being sick was a much better thing to be among us than being crazy. This is because it is an im-portant mitzvah—a good deed—prescribed in the Torah to help those suffering from illness and disease. A Jew who eases the suffering of the ill receives an assured place in paradise; his heavenly reward is immeasurable. But in the Torah it says nothing about helping crazy people.

If Nachum got sick, of course the disease would have to be a serious one. It could not be just any old cold or strep. It was best if it was a dreadful thing, an affliction that could lead to death, like cancer or the bubonic plague. Then everyone would be nice to my mother. They would offer her a hand, they would offer my father their money, and every morning our teacher would announce Nachum's name during prayers. All my classmates would treat me kindly. They'd give me first choice from their snacks, and at recess would allow me an ex-tra turn at every game. It would be different from how things were now, with my friends telling one another my secrets and adults staring at my family, half in suspicion, half in fear, from a careful distance.

*   *   *

My father paced back and forth in the kitchen. His fist came down hard on the counter and table. He shouted in rage, his words thundering through the house, until the walls of my room trembled.

I hid in my blanket box, my hands tightly over my ears. My sisters had run downstairs to the basement. But my mother wasn't scared. Her voice hurtled along the hallway from the kitchen to my room.

"*No!*" she said in Hebrew, in a terrible voice. "My child is not disposable!"

My father shouted, "You are dreaming! It's *hopeless!* Every expert has said so!"

"They are ignorant! So I should be hopeless? Do you know how many doctors I haven't seen yet?"

I listened to my mother fighting for Nachum, and could not understand her. Why didn't she give him away? Why didn't she leave him somewhere—anywhere—and run as fast as she could in the other direction? Whyever would anyone *want* such a child?

I covered my head with a blanket and waited for the yelling to stop. I had never heard my parents fight like this before; I had never heard their voices filled with so much raging pain. What if Nachum tore at them until there was nothing left? What if my father left the house and never returned?

Would he take me with him? Would I want to go? Would my mother take Nachum and tell the rest of us to leave?

In the end, my father strode out of the house, leaving a silence like a heavy fog. Slowly, I crept out of the box. I opened the door. Then I turned back, curled up in my bed, and stared at an open book, thinking.

When my mother had been to Israel last summer, she prayed at my ancestors' holy graves high in the hills outside Jerusalem. My aunts who lived nearby prayed there too. They prayed often for Nachum. Even the rebbe had blessed my mother when she came to him, saying that all would be well, amen.

All was not.

The neighbor a few houses down once told the mailman, as I tried pulling Nachum away from the stones he'd dug up in her garden, that only God could understand the strange thing that was that child. I did not know if God could understand the strange thing that was my brother. Maybe He had not meant to make it happen this way, and thought it strange too. But that could not be. God did not make mistakes, which meant that He had done it on purpose. And if He had done it on purpose, He could undo it on purpose. But He did not.

I had heard Mrs. Rosen talking about my brother when I played at her house with her daughter, Shany, a girl my age. She told someone on the phone that such a boy should have been put away long ago, because a child like that turned the whole house upside down.

This was true. Nachum turned our whole house upside down. I had heard the words "put away" several times, though I'd never known exactly what they meant. But if other people—all good fathers and mothers—did it, I was sure it was just fine. It did not matter who had broken the boy—angels or men. It did not even matter exactly what this meant; such a child just had to be put away.

The next morning when I woke up, there was a huge bouquet of flowers on the living room table. In the evening, when my father came home from work, it was as if my parents had never fought. They spoke in their regular voices. But I knew it wasn't over, that the screaming would happen again. Because Nachum wasn't better; he was worse.

Thirty

June 1, 1989
Inside my blanket box, holding a book of psalms:

"*Shir La'ma'alos Mimaamakim...* From the depths of despair I call to you, O Lord, take my brother away... *Adonay tiftach nah, Adonay mi ya'amod...* My master, open my eyes, who is like you, O Lord, who can take my brother away... *Yachel yisroel el adonay...* Please, please, please, Hashem, make him go far away."

June 2
Same box, holding psalms:

"*Chaneni Adonay Ki Umlal Ani...* Have mercy upon me, O Lord, for my brother makes me weak... *Refaenu Adonay Ki Nivhalu Atzomuy...* O Lord, heal me of my troubles, for my brother is still here... *Nafshi Nivhala M'od Ad Masay*...But thou, O Lord, how long will he be around? Please make him go somewhere away.

"I promise never to say an evil word of others; I will never read another fairy tale. I will never eat candies from Kathy even if they're kosher, but only if the Lord will receive my prayer..."

June 3
Still in my box, with psalms:

"Dear God, master of this world. Just take Nachum already. I am tired of saying psalms in a box."

That evening, in between prayers and pleas, I went up to Kathy's and watched TV with her. Afterward, I did not repent.

Thirty-One

In the end, it was Nachum who went.

It was right at the start of July, a few weeks before I turned nine years old. We were up in the Catskill Mountains for the long summer months with thousands of ultraorthodox families.

In the bungalow colony where we stayed, we ran and played among the clusters of tiny, broken-down cabins—our very own paradise. It was cooler up there, in the green fields and wide-open spaces. There we were free, far from the steaming city and its narrow backyards.

I loved the bungalow my father had built for us right on top of the colony's hill. From our porch, we could see across the sparkling lake, its sun-dipped water twinkling. Along the dirt roads winding through the back of our colony, Blimi, Chaya Sarah, and I explored. We played catch a thief around the old oak trees that lined the hill. Where the colony ended and the forest began stood a glorious colonial home at least two hundred years old; it was where the Feinbergs stayed with their thirteen children. Underneath the sagging arches that held up the back of the house, Blimi and I had a hideaway place, our exclusive, secret club. It was there we decided that the twins, Leah and Ruchela, could not join us in our club just because in the city they were my only neighbors. Here they were not.

A week and a half after we arrived in the Catskills, my mother packed a suitcase, or maybe two, and left the bungalow colony with Nachum while I was in day camp. I did not see her for five days. Seventeen-year-old Bailah stayed with us until she returned. Like all the other fathers, my father stayed in the city during the week to work. He came up only for Shabbos.

I liked Bailah because she was kind and patient. She fed us macaroni and cheese all week long. "Your mother will come back very soon," she told me, but she said nothing about Nachum. And so, just like that, my brother disappeared again, nine months after he'd come back. One day, he was with us in the mountains, and the next day, he was gone. This time, Yitzy said, it was for good. Nachum had gone back to live with my aunt and uncle on Rabbi Holy Man Street. He was never coming home again.

I told the twins what Yitzy had said, and then I told Blimi. But she only answered, "Oh. Could I have two Hello Kitty stickers? Please? Just one?" I said no. It wasn't my fault she didn't have a collection.

On the second of the five nights, Bailah let me sleep in Blimi's bungalow, which was down the hill from ours. But in the middle of the night, I woke up because of the ghosts howling frightfully right outside my window and walked back home in the dark.

Blimi ran after me, saying that I was being silly.

"It's just the wind," she said, but I walked right on.

I was turning nine in three weeks, I said, and I knew the difference between the wind and ghosts.

Blimi hurried after me until we reached the top of the hill. She tried to persuade me to come back, but when she saw that I would not, she said she'd come with me. She wasn't going back down the dark hill alone. So Blimi and I tiptoed into my bungalow and fell asleep in my bed together, huddled on my narrow mattress.

Then it was early morning. In my dream, I heard a pounding and a shaking and felt myself falling, falling down a steep mountain to nowhere. Then a hard push, a loud voice, and I opened my eyes. Blimi's mother's angry face loomed over us. I could vaguely see Bailah blinking her tired eyes somewhere behind her. I stared at them blankly.

"Are you crazy?" Blimi's mother was yelling. "We were looking for you all over! I almost called the police! How can you just disappear like that?"

We had forgotten to tell her that we had left the bungalow in the middle of the night.

Blimi sat up, blinking. I rubbed my eyes and told Mrs. Krieger about the ghosts. But she did not want to hear about ghosts. Instead, she shouted at us for a long time. She said that we were thoughtless, feckless, irresponsible, and that she'd never let us sleep in the same house again. Then she marched Blimi right back down the hill.

Thirty-Two

For weeks after coming back home, my strong mother wept, grieving for my brother. I'd hear her in the early mornings, talking with Aunt Itta on the phone. I'd hear her late at night and sometimes after school, crying behind the closed door of her room.

My mother wept. Long after my aunt had hung up, after my uncle was off the line, she'd cradle the phone in her hand, as if she could not let go of the people on the other end of the line. There was pain in her eyes and sorrow in her movements as she cleaned and cooked. After dark, she wrote long letters in Hebrew, the graceful curves of her words filling sheet after sheet of paper—letters for my aunt, for my uncle, maybe for my brother. At dawn, when I woke up, I'd hear her weeping again.

It was September, and we were back home in the city, but I did not thank God for taking Nachum away. This was not a miracle. How could He answer a prayer in such a terrible way?

Maybe Nachum was gone, but so was my mother, half of her heart still in Jerusalem.

Nachum had not wanted my mother to leave him. He had held on to her hands, his fingers clasped around her wrists, the day she was to go to the airport. When my aunt pulled him away, he had thrown himself on the floor, his arms locked around my mother's ankle in an iron grip. He had cried frantically, "Ima! Ima! Ima! Ima!," because he did not want to be left there, alone.

My mother wept because she could not forget his tears, because she wanted my brother back in New York, where he could never belong. Sometimes my father spoke with her, and I could hear his voice behind the door of their room. In Israel, he said, my brother could get the help he needed. In Israel, my aunt and uncle and their two daughters, who were older, could care for him in a way that it was impossible for us to do at home, not with five young children under the age of thirteen, not with five little ones who needed a mother too.

Things had already quieted down at home. Aside from my mother's sadness, we were, once again, a normal family. Apart from her sighs, we were just plain and ordinary, no different than my neighbors and friends. My father never thundered anymore; my parents barely fought. My cousin Shaindel even slept over at our house when her mother went away. It was peaceful, the way it used to be before my brother had come back.

And maybe that's how we started to forget that we had a brother on the other side of the ocean. Maybe that's how all of us, except my mother, forgot that Nachum had ever lived with us at home. Rivky too. She did not say his name even once. Because it was easy to forget a brother who lived that far away. It was easy to forget a brother with the start of the school year, homework, new teachers, and old schoolyard rivalries; with Chaya Sarah's arm newly broken, textbooks suddenly piled high, and the new red swing set my father had built at the side of our house. It was just plain easy to forget. And maybe that's why, a few weeks afterward, my mother called a family meeting.

All of us kids were expected to be there.

We sat dutifully around the glass table in the living room, waiting. Yitzy stared ahead with a serious expression. Miri sucked her thumb and swung her foot impatiently. My mother, in the head chair, looked at each of us. Then she began.

"Do you know why I called this meeting?" she asked.

Yitzy's eyes focused on the wall. Rivky's lips pressed worriedly together. Miri, still sucking her thumb, stared wide-eyed at my mother. I looked down, through the glass table, at a lone ant crawling across the floor. There was quiet all around.

"Can any of you tell me why I called this meeting?" my mother asked, but still we were silent. A minute passed. Then another. Finally, she spoke.

"It's been weeks since Nachum left," she said. "Doesn't anyone here want to know anything about your brother?"

I pressed my tongue down on the glass table. It was a fun thing to do. The saliva on the glass made a different pattern with each press. My mother's eyes settled on the top of my head. I did not see, but I could feel them boring right through my scalp. I sat straight up, my tongue back in my mouth. I could see the pain in her eyes.

She waited.

"Is there nothing, then, nothing you want to know about Nachum? How he's doing? How he feels? Is he better? Is he worse? Does he talk? Does he cry?"

Stillness. Her eyebrows furrowed as she looked at each of us in turn. She could not understand.

"Have you already forgotten that you have another brother, your own flesh and blood? Have you forgotten that there is a boy who lives in Israel, and that no matter how long he's away, he's still ours?"

She stared at us, as if trying to read our minds, and I was glad that she could not. Because it would be a terrible sin to tell my mother the truth and to make her heart hurt even more. It would be a terrible sin to tell her that we did not miss this kind of brother, and that there had been times I had hoped he'd just die and leave us alone.

Stupid, tapping angel. Stupid, crazy love. I wanted nothing to do with any of it anymore. And that's why I had prayed for an end, but my mother had no idea that God had listened, that maybe this was why Nachum was taken away. I could never tell her how long I'd been asking for this terrible thing, and how much of it was perhaps my fault. Yes, I had prayed for a kind and good death for my brother, but still. Anybody would be horrified, especially if he really turned out to be a higher soul. If I were God, I'd keep things much more simple and straightforward. Then I wouldn't have to listen to so many tearful prayers.

My mother was looking at me, and I sat up straight as though I was listening to the things she was saying, things about Nachum and his new school, and the therapy they were trying. Then she asked if we had questions. We did not. She said that we'd have a family meeting like this once a month, because she did not want us to forget that we had a brother.

Miri, her thumb still sucked up in her mouth, kicked me in the knee just then, from all that foot swinging under the table. I would have kicked her back hard, but my mother, the pain still lingering in her silence, said that the family meeting was over. We could go.

I ran out of the house as fast as my bruised knee could carry me to catch the new swings before Miri and Rivky did. I loved the swing set, which my father had put up for us as a surprise. He had built it just the week earlier, after days and days of our begging. He had been saying that he would do it, but only in the spring, six long months away. But then one afternoon the twins and I raced down the two blocks from their house to mine, and there, like a miracle from the sky, was the half-built swing set.

My father had laughed when he saw me running up, prancing giddily under the bright red frame. The twins and I had waited impatiently, watching him work. Then, when it stood solid and steady, the two new swings dangling carefree in the breeze, we had jumped on the seats and pushed one another high, taking turns flying in the wind.

I pumped my legs hard now, feeling the rush of air against my face. Miri sat on the swing next to me, pumping her legs, her thumb somehow still in her mouth.

I still felt terrible about my mother's sorrow. It wasn't that I'd forgotten. But it was hard feeling bad with a swing set so new and red. I promised myself that I'd feel terrible again, but in a little while. On a different day. Some other time. Just not right then.

Thirty-Three

Later that week, I played with Sammy. Sammy was a dog.

Sammy the dog belonged to Diana, a gentile lady who lived two blocks down.

Sammy and Diana had been walking past my block every day at three o'clock, but for a long time, I didn't know them, just as I didn't know most of my neighbors. As I've said, we did not befriend such kinds. But then one day, two things happened: Diana walked Sammy at four o'clock instead of three, and I came off the school van just as they passed by. So I nearly stepped on Sammy's paw before I noticed him, and that he was a dog.

A dog.

Dropping my schoolbag, I ran, screaming, down the block, never once looking back. I ran until I could not breathe and stumbled behind a neighbor's bush. I crouched there, cowering in a tangle of bristly branches, begging God for mercy. There was a dog out there. A dirty dog—one of those ferocious creatures with teeth like knives that hunted down Jews in the forests of Germany and Poland, ripping their flesh off their bones. Good Jews didn't like dogs. We stayed far away.

I knelt, trembling, listening for any sound. There were only the distant sounds of speeding cars. I peered carefully through the bush. The neighbor and her dog were gone. Stumbling out, I ran back home.

But the next day they were there again, the old lady and her terrifying dog. This time, I saw them before they reached our house. I fled up the steps and I stared down at them from the porch. Good heavens, dear Lord of the universe, those things were everywhere.

I eyed the dog, my heart beating hard. I took in its panting, hanging-out tongue, its dark fur and wagging tail. I could see the old lady smile hesitantly.

"I'm sorry," she said. "I didn't mean to scare you. Sammy is a gentle dog. He won't hurt you." And she petted the creature, stroking its back as it looked at me with its demonic eyes.

Well, I thought from my great distance, she's safe because she's a goy. Dogs don't bite goyim.

The old lady smiled softly now, her eyes creasing under the floral scarf she wore on her head.

"Do you want to pet him?" she asked.

Pet him? Whyever would I want to do *that*?

I shook my head quickly and half smiled back. The old lady nodded. Then she and the dog slowly walked away.

The next day, I sat on the grass inside our gate, so when the old lady came I was still safe, a full two yards away. I watched her and the dog walk slowly toward our corner house.

She was an old lady like any other, her beige trench coat pulled tightly around her thin frame, the colorful floral scarf tied loosely over her head. Why, if not for the dog on the long leather leash, one could barely tell she was a gentile.

She stopped when she saw me. I stared at her curiously.

"Sit, Sammy," she said, and the dog did.

I looked at Sammy warily. He stared patiently back at me.

"What's your name?" the old lady asked.

I didn't answer.

"My name is Diana," she said. "I live there." She pointed toward East Second Street. "And Sammy's my old dog. I bought him when he was just a wee pup. Now look how big he's got."

I stood up and stepped toward the fence. The dog shifted his weight. I stepped back twice.

"Does it bite?" I asked. Because all dogs bite. My friends even said so.

Diana chuckled. "Oh, no," she said. "Sammy's an old dog and very gentle. Even cats aren't afraid of him."

And suddenly, like that, I was curious. I wanted to know what a dog felt like. So I stuck a hand through a hole in the fence and touched him with one finger. Then two. I was surprised. His fur wasn't rough. It was warm and smooth and had a silky feel. All the while, he didn't move, just sat on the sidewalk like an oversize stuffed animal, staring ahead, comfortable and calm. I pulled my hand back in. Then I looked at Diana. She looked back at me. Suddenly, I felt silly for having been so nervous. I laughed out loud.

*   *   *

I played with Sammy almost every day after that. I played with him until I wasn't scared at all. I liked Diana because if she weren't a goy, she would definitely have been a Jew. She looked like any old aunt, with her large gentle eyes, wrinkly skin, and orthopedic old-lady shoes. The dog gave her away, of course, but still, she was a nice gentile to have around. In fact, her late husband's father's mother, she told me one day, had been a Jew, and when she was a young girl somewhere down in Tennessee, she had had a good friend named Ruth whose father was a rabbi.

I told this to Rivky when she said that there were too many goyim in my life, and that no decent Jewish girl was friends with a dog. I told her that Sammy was a different kind of dog, one who did not bite Jews, and that maybe Diana's great-great-grandmother had been a secret Jew, but never told anyone. Kathy, I reassured her, was a good goy too. The proof was the kosher candy she always kept in her closet just for me. But Rivky said that candy was no proof. The goyim only showed their true colors in times of pogroms and wars.

I told her that it couldn't be. Kathy was one of the righteous gentiles, as was Diana, and they were definitely not like evil goyim. Rivky said that there was no way I could know that, and that just because I liked them, it didn't make them righteous. Their *nice* was fake, she said, and I was sinning by trusting them.

I threw a marker at Rivky, exasperated.

"But I do not trust gentiles," I shouted. "I know all gentiles are evil, stupidhead! *Except* for Diana and Kathy. Only the two of them!"

All gentiles were bad, our teachers had taught us, but there were some exceptions—it says so in the midrash. In every generation, it is written, there are thirty-six righteous gentiles who are not like the others. Those are the gentiles who save Jews during a holocaust, who help Jewish children escape a pogrom. Those are the goyim who do not carry hate inside, because they have real souls.

Kathy and Diana were not only not evil; they were not even regular gentiles. I could be friends with them as much as I pleased, because they were the kind that were good inside, and one day when a holocaust would finally come, my stupid sister would see. Our sages had foretold.

So I played with Sammy every day after school. Then I'd go up to Kathy's and we'd talk. But I never repented for it again. I didn't need to. Because it really was a wonder how lucky I was: God had planned it so that two out of the thirty-six righteous gentiles on earth lived right next to me.

Thirty-Four

A few weeks after the family meeting, my mother left for Israel. Packed inside her luggage were toys and sweets enough to last a boy for a year.

This was how things would be now. With my brother in Israel for good, my mother would be going away more often, flying to Jerusalem every few months—at least three or four times a year. She was going to see my brother, she had explained to us, to stay with him for a while, and to meet with psychologists and experts trying to find a cure.

I didn't mind my mother's going to Israel, because for the two weeks she'd be gone, I'd stay at Blimi's house. Blimi said that we'd have more fun than in the bungalow colony, and that she'd show me how to turn a blanket into a tent. All my siblings were to be sent away, scattered among family and friends. We could not stay at home with my mother overseas and my father working from early morning until night.

In the days before she left, toys in boxes of every shape

and size had begun piling up in the corner of my parents' bedroom, as well as shopping bags filled with sweaters and robes—gifts for my brother and aunt. In my mother's carry-on were sweets: Peanut Chews, fruit leather, Chew Chews, and other treats that my brother loved but that could not be found in Jerusalem. Then, the evening before the flight, she packed everything—her own belongings last—into her suitcases.

I bounced on these suitcases, pushing down on them so she could pull the zippers shut. Then, as my father dragged them down the steps and into the cab, I kissed my mother goodbye. She hugged me tightly and said I should behave.

"I will, I will," I said. "You're choking me."

After my mother left, I sat next to my father on the couch. It was quiet in the house, my siblings already with friends and family, and the empty rooms all around me echoed in strange silence.

"You von't see me dis whole week," my father said. "You going to mees me?"

I laid my head on the arm of the couch, my feet on my father's lap. I thought some.

"A little," I said.

My father laughed. He pulled off my shoe and tickled me. I yelped and kicked his hands away. Then he sighed. He leaned back, his arms behind his head, and sighed again. Then he looked up at the ceiling, lost in thought.

"Are you happy Nachum is not here?" I asked, because suddenly I needed to know.

My father sat up straight, like a soldier. His hands fell

silently onto his lap, and his eyes went very still. He did not answer my question. Then, with his right hand, he stroked the end of his beard, wrapping the thick curls around his forefinger over and around again. As if I had never asked the question, he leaned back once more, staring up at the chandelier.

"I'm happy," I said, reassuringly. "I don't like Nachum either."

My father did not move this time, but kept his eyes on the hanging crystals, his face unreadable as a sphinx. I sat up quietly and said I was going to my room. I did not ask again.

I put my fairy-tale book in the back of my schoolbag. Then, after a few minutes, my father said that it was time to leave. He picked up my little suitcase, the one my mother had packed the night before, and I carried my schoolbag. Then my father drove me to Blimi's house in Borough Park.

We drove under the bridge, past the train tracks that separated Borough Park from Flatbush. We stopped at Goldberg's grocery on Eighteenth Avenue and bought two chocolate bars, one for me and one for Blimi. Also a pack of gum, in case I was homesick.

It would start to snow soon, the man on the radio said. The cold was rushing toward the city. Outside the car window, the wind blew at the trees, and the bare branches swung playfully. Soon it would be Chanukah again, and my father had promised me a gold bracelet. In two weeks, my mother would return from Jerusalem with chocolates and colorful dreidels.

At last, out my window I saw Blimi waving excitedly, running down her block toward our car. Mrs. Krieger, standing on the steps of the house, called her back, but then she saw us and smiled. She walked quickly down the path, pulling the kerchief down over her forehead, tucking in the hairs straying out along her neckline. She stood at the edge of the driveway as my father parked the car.

I opened the door, feeling small and shy, as my father took my little suitcase and put it down by the entrance door. Blimi's mother, still smiling, told me to run inside now; Blimi would show me the room we'd sleep in. But I didn't want to go in yet. I wanted to watch my father go.

I waited for my father to finish speaking with Mrs. Krieger, and then waited as he settled back into the driver's seat. He turned the key in the ignition and put his hands on the wheel. Then my father turned to me, waved, and smiled.

I watched him drive away. I waved at the blue minivan until it grew smaller and smaller, until it turned a corner and was gone. Then I went inside the plain redbrick house, Blimi's mother behind me. I heard Blimi shouting my name from the back of the house. She said that I should come already— quick. My suitcase was already there, in her room, and she was now jumping on her bed.

My suitcase lay open, my clothes all over the floor. Blimi had found the chocolate bar. She threw me a piece, shouting "Catch!," and said I should come and jump with her. I did, and we giggled and laughed, jumping higher and higher on the creaking springs until her mother told us to stop.

I didn't mind staying so far from home—I really didn't. Because we'd have fun at Blimi's. She'd teach me how to turn a blanket into a tent. At night, we'd have ice cream and read my fairy-tale book, while her parents and siblings slept. We'd read about the beauty and the beast, the princess and the frog, and I'd explain to Blimi how they were just like the Tales of Tzaddikim, in which the prince, I meant the saint, was always disguised as a beast, I meant a pauper, or sometimes as a madman, as he wandered the kingdoms and forests of distant lands. And how miracles were like magic, and magic just like miracles.

That night, Blimi and I read our favorite stories. We read until we fell asleep, way past midnight. In the morning, Blimi's mother came into the room to wake us, and that's when, of course, she saw my book, the one we'd fallen asleep on.

Mrs. Krieger made me put the book back into my suitcase, and my suitcase deep under the bed. She said that she wanted both Blimi and me to promise that we would not take the book out again to read, not in her house. Blimi and I promised because, really, we had no choice. But behind our backs, we crossed our fingers.

Part IV

Thirty-Five

Four years later
July 1, 1993
El Al airlines, thirty-five thousand feet above the Atlantic Ocean

The plane shook like a rattling toy in the great, angry sky. The captain's gravelly voice crackled over the speakers:

"Attention all passengers. Attention all passengers. This is your captain speaking. We are currently experiencing minor turbulence. Please remain seated until further notice."

This was it. I knew it. My first time in five years on a plane, and already I was dying. I clutched my travel-size book of psalms and gripped the armrest. My last moments on earth. A flight attendant walked briskly up the aisle, her crisp smile pasted across her face. Her head turned left, then right, left, then right, robotically checking each passenger's seat.

"Please fasten your seat belts," she said. "Sir, your seat belt..."
She stopped to help the man seated across the aisle from me.

But there was no fooling me. It was over; I knew.

Turbulence? That's what all captains said when things went
wrong, the instant before the plane crashed right out of the
heavens. What else could he say? "Attention all passengers.
Don't bother with the seat belts. We are all going to die."

We were definitely going to die.

I eyed the elderly woman next to me. Oblivious to the
doom that awaited, she never moved her eyes off the big center screen. Her face remained steady under her short, blond
wig, a string of pearls peeking out from beneath her double
chin. Death was all around us, and she was watching the news.

I had never wanted to go to Israel. I should have been on
my way to summer camp like every normal thirteen-year-old.
But my mother had said absolutely not.

"There will be no camp this year. Not this time. Not after
four years." Four years since I'd last seen my brother. I wished
I was on my way to camp.

Six summers had passed since I had boarded the El Al airlines
flight clutching Yitzy's hand and Nachum's pinky finger. I had
been nearly seven years old, and for ten hours, legs dangling
off the passenger seat, I'd imagined that I was on the wings of
an eagle.

But this was no eagle, this flying machine, with its
narrow seats, crowded aisles, and pumped-in oxygen, which

left a nasty, sterile taste in my mouth. There were too many people here: snoring men, crying infants, and impatient stewardesses, their glued-on smiles wilting away in the stormy sky.

It was too late to go back. Once on the plane, there was no walking off, not before we had reached my mother's planned destination. And when I reached it, whether I liked it or not, I was going to meet my brother.

"Nachum is different now," my mother had said proudly. "He's almost a man. And he wants to meet his sister."

"You won't recognize him," Aunt Tziporah had added. "He's not the child he used to be."

My sister Rivky said nothing, and my brother Yitzy shrugged. Miri, even Avrumi—they had all gone but me. I had spent my summers in the Catskills instead, all eight weeks in the colony or at sleepaway camp. After age ten or eleven, camp was where most girls spent their summers, and for a long time my mother agreed. Until she did not.

"You wouldn't believe how he talks," she told me, and I had pretended to believe her. "He can hold entire conversations." But when I thought of Nachum, I saw only flailing hands.

"You wouldn't believe how he can read," said my aunt. "He's a real mensch, a proud young man." But when I looked out our backyard window, I saw Nachum, hunched over and alone, far from the playing children.

"Things have changed," said my mother, and I had nodded

as though I was listening. But inside my head I was somewhere else, anywhere but Israel.

This time, the suitcases lying open on the dining room table
had been mine. I would be the one handing my brother the
gifts and sweets that bulged from every corner of the bag.
My mother had hugged me tightly, tears in her eyes. She had
checked my carry-on, again and again.

"Your passport is here, the credit card here, the cash right
here, and the airport security—remember: you answer them
short and to the point. No diddling or extra answers. And
don't take a package from anyone! I don't care if he looks like
the chief rabbi of Israel..." On the right side of the carry-on
were three packs of gum, and on the left side solution for my
ears for landing. Because when I was a baby, I'd had a terrible
ear infection that had gone on for weeks. So you never knew.
It could help.

"Call me as soon as you land, Menuchah, you hear? Aunt
Zahava will be waiting for you at the terminal. Remember
what she looks like? Remember? Are you sure?"

Four years is a long time for a brother to be gone, always hovering in the background, just around the corner of our lives.
Four years is a long time to know a brother who is gone only
from the fragments my mother brought home every time she

came back from Israel. There was the framed painting hanging like a memorial on the wall; the carefully preserved letter with his first, illegible written words; the Judaica candlesticks formed out of wax and the mosaics that she said he'd made. Lost bits of memories were scattered across our halls. Nachum had stopped being real the day he left home.

My mother had spoken of Nachum often, and I had listened because I had to, but as if to some faraway legend about a crazy boy. Oh, I felt for the people in the narrative, for their pain and futile struggle, but not too much. That's just how it is with legends. The thing about this one was that it unfolded all around me, characters wandering in and out from the pages of their story and into mine, telling me things, explaining, wanting to hear my thoughts, unable to know that I had no part in their drama, that this was just some legend about a tragic boy.

The tragedy and the boy lived across the sea. His mother traveled there often, leaving her other children behind to visit him. This mother said that her boy was not crazy, that he was only lost in a labyrinth that had trapped his mind. If she could just break into the labyrinth, she would find her hostage boy and bring him home.

There was also a father in the story who was tall and very silent. He did not try to stop the mother from going. Instead, he gave large sums of money for the trips across the sea, as if, even in his silence, he really believed they might do some good.

For years the mother searched. She searched for anyone who could tell her how to find her lost boy. She traveled from city to city, from one expert to another, but to no avail. No one knew of any labyrinth. Mostly they said it didn't exist, that there was no boy inside to find.

There was the doctor who thought it was ADHD, but it turned out it was not. There was the psychiatrist who declared it to be a psychosis, but who could not say what kind it was. A physician in Manhattan said it was a brain chemical the boy lacked, one that could be supplied by medication, but the medication left the boy nauseous and ill, and the chemical was still missing.

A holy man said it was the doings of the evil eye. Special prayers and sacred water would force it out. So he prayed and chanted and sprinkled the boy with water, but though the boy got very wet, the evil eye stayed inside. And then there was the renowned professor who told the mother to stop trying. In his wide and spacious Manhattan office, way up on the twenty-seventh floor, he held an onion in the palm of his hand.

"The boy is like an onion," he said from across the cherry-wood desk. "You peel off one layer, and another. And then, just when you think you're done, you find another layer underneath. Layers and layers of problems..."

He put the onion down, so the mother should see.

"You are trying to find an apple in a child that's an onion," he said, and he told her to go back home. Put the child away. Forget about him. Such children were lost forever. They could never be found.

The mother left the office. She took the elevator back down twenty-six floors. For days she wept whenever she saw an onion. Then she continued with her search.

Time passed. The boy was now eight years old. The school he attended overseas for children with special needs and other general disabilities said he was hopeless. Their other students— Down syndrome, developmentally delayed—all progressed in the program, but not this child. This boy's disability was a strange one, not of the general kind. They did not want him any longer, they said. The mother and silent father paid vast sums of money just so the school should keep trying.

Then one day, someone told the mother about a last-hope psychologist in Jerusalem, another expert he had heard of, and she sighed. "This one is different," he said. "This psychologist is known as the one who tests untestable children. She diagnoses only the worst cases. Take your son to her. If anyone can diagnose him, she can. And if she can't—well, then..."

This is how the lost boy and his mother arrived at the office of the last-hope psychologist, Dr. Cory Shulman, known for testing untestable children, boys and girls who could not be found.

The doctor sat with the crazy boy for an hour, maybe two. Outside, in the reception area, the mother waited apprehensively. She read weekly magazines and insert advertisements. She stood up and sat back down. She paced around the small office, listening to the sounds behind the wall. Finally, the doctor came out. The boy shuffled behind her. He sat down on a chair, staring straight ahead.

Dr. Shulman turned to the mother, asking her to come into her office. She asked her many questions about the boy. She wanted to know everything about him. What had he been like as an infant? As a toddler? With the siblings? In each school? The doctor filled out many papers, checking lists and scribbling things down. Then she sent them both away.

"Thank you for coming," she said. "I will call you, God willing, tomorrow."

The evening came and went. The night crept by, ever so slowly, and finally dawn came. The mother sat up in the silent apartment, unable to sleep. What if this last-hope doctor did not know either? What if this doctor could not test her untestable child? Wherever would she go then?

But early that morning, the psychologist called. She asked the mother to come to her office again. The boy stayed home with an aunt and uncle and watched through the window as the white cab drove away, his mother sitting in the backseat.

In the office, the mother sat across the crowded desk from the last-hope expert, who had a small stack of papers in front of her. Then at last Dr. Shulman told the mother that she had evaluated the boy's tests, and that in the labyrinth she had found a diagnosis.

"Nachum is a child with autistic tendencies," the mother heard her say. "Nachum meets the criteria of a condition known as autism spectrum disorder. This is a neurological condition that he was born with."

She paused and looked closely at the mother.

"Your son is autistic," she said, and then waited to see if the mother had absorbed this.

The mother stared at the doctor. She stared at the papers that Dr. Shulman held out. "Autistic," she said. "What's autistic?"

And that's how the first story goes.

*   *   *

I kicked the seat in front of me, trying to stretch out and sleep. The man in it turned around, glaring. It was inhumane, this business of sleeping in a flying can of sardines. I sat back up, exhausted. The seat belt sign glowed red. The plane shuddered. I looked out the porthole at the dark outside, where the bullying winds pushed the aircraft to and fro.

Before I had left New York, Kathy told me that she'd switch places with me in less than a minute. Who didn't want to go to the Holy Land? I said, "Okay, let's do it." Kathy had laughed. She said that she had always wanted to visit Israel, the place where Jesus walked, but it was too expensive. When I told her that I really didn't want to go—people died in planes all the time—she said that I was safe.

"Don't worry, Menu'hah. God loves you, and He takes good care of planes going to His land. You're gonna love it there. You wait and see—you won't wanna come back anytime soon."

She also promised that Jesus was going to watch over me from her prayers, and that my God would watch over me from my prayers, so that between the two of them, my flight was foolproof.

But I hadn't wanted Jesus to watch over me. I just wanted my own God to masterfully change my mother's grand plan and get me off the plane. Or at least stop the turbulence.

*   *   *

The elderly woman next to me asked me a question, and I turned to her, startled. She had finished watching the news.

"Are you going for a family wedding?" she repeated, smiling at my startled expression.

I shook my head.

"No," I said. "I'm going…I'm going…"

Where *was* I going? To visit my crazy brother?

No. Definitely not. Not with the questions that would follow. The person I was going to visit was some other sibling, a plain just-any-kind-of-brother, who happened to live overseas.

But elderly ladies had a way, I knew. They always wanted more information.

So which school is he in? she'd inquire. How old is he? Oh, and what is the name of this just-any-kind-of-brother? And why Israel, with so many good schools in New York? And I'd have to remember every lie, and the order in which I told them, all for one impossible question.

I changed my mind. I was certainly going for a family wedding.

"It's my mother's youngest sister," I explained. "But mostly a bar mitzvah. My first cousin's. He's the oldest so it's a big deal.…Yes, we're very close. He's coming to New York for my bas mitzvah. I mean he came already—last year."

Huh?

But the lady did not delve. She chatted mostly about herself and the married son she was visiting who had just had his seventh child. We talked some until the turbulence finally stopped and I fell asleep.

*   *   *

When I woke up, the plane was dropping out of the sky, along with my intestines. We were landing, the captain announced. All passengers were to be seated immediately.

I bent over quickly, burying my head between my knees. A flash of nausea passed through me. I covered my ears, forcing myself to take deep breaths. I offered God my last prayers.

It was a mystery to me, how my mother did this four times a year, flying from New York to Israel and back, be it winter, Passover, or war.

When she had gone two years before, it had been in the middle of a war. A short war, only five weeks long, but still, who flew? During war, people stayed firmly on the ground, especially after Saddam Hussein promised the final destruction of Israel. When the first Scud missile had hit the previous month, no one knew when it would end, and my mother wouldn't wait. I could see it in her eyes. Let fire and brimstone rain down on the land. She would be in Israel to see her son on Tuesday, the day she'd promised him she would come.

Missiles streaked red across the Mediterranean sky the day my mother flew to Israel in February 1991 on a plane carrying her, two other passengers, and one hundred and fifty empty seats. In the airport in Tel Aviv, a soldier handed them masks to protect them from poison gas. In the terminal, the conveyor belt rolled around, empty but for three suitcases. Outside, a lone taxi waited.

To Jerusalem, he said, it was double the price or nothing. There was a war.

For ten days my mother stayed in Israel as the country came to a halt. The war complicated things, with the sirens going and the missiles overhead. Cousin Ayalah had to keep her hands tightly over Nachum's ears as Uncle Zev carried him down to the sealed room, a bombproof shelter underground, while his body convulsed and he shrieked in agony, trying to stop the sounds. This was because Nachum did not know that there was a war around him, did not know about a country called Iraq, only that the sirens cut into his brain like a drill saw.

The war, with the fear it inspired and the constant radio warnings, complicated other things too, such as the meetings with Dr. Shulman in her office, and sometimes in a sealed room in her building. She was preparing the documents and arguments needed to convince the Ministry of Education's placement committee to approve a spot for Nachum in the program for autistic children.

When my mother boarded a plane to return home in mid-February, missiles still streaked across the sky. It was shortly after she returned to Brooklyn that Aunt Itta called with the news: the placement committee had approved. And for the first time since Nachum left, I saw my mother really smile.

Thirty-Six

Ben Gurion Airport, Tel Aviv

There were soldiers everywhere. They wandered through the airport in their laced-up boots and uniforms, automatic weapons slung casually over their shoulders.

I dragged my suitcase behind me, looking up for an exit. There were signs all around me, green arrows indicating arrivals, departures, and ground transportation. I followed two fast-talking passengers, walking close behind them as they strode through corridors and doors, past escalators and restrooms.

At the little security booth, the man peered gravely at my passport, and then at me. Beyond the passport control booths, I could see the luggage riding on the conveyor belt in the cavernous baggage claim area. The man in the booth stamped my passport. "Welcome to Israel," he said.

I found my suitcases, heaved them onto the cart, and pushed it down the never-ending corridors. Three miles of bright white waxed floor must have passed in front of my eyes before I finally saw the gate for customs. A blur of unfamiliar faces looked out at me: men with large *kippas,* women in jeans, girls in miniskirts and tank tops standing by boys with shaved heads and side curls. Jews, Jews, a bewildering array of Jews. I searched the crowd. A taxi driver held a sign with a name; a long-bearded rabbi stood, holy book in hand; a soldier waited impatiently, a dozen roses in his arms.

Aunt Zahava spotted me first. From somewhere I heard "Menuchah! Menuchah! *Puh!* Here!" and turned toward the sound. She was waving frantically, pushing her way through the crowd. My mother's older sister was still tall and slender, just as I remembered. A shoulder-length wig framed her face.

"Oh, Menuchah," she exclaimed, embracing me tightly. "You look just like your mother!" She grabbed my suitcase in one hand, straightening the collar of my shirt with the other.

"You must be so ti—" she began, just as a woman shoved us aside, rushing happily at another who had just arrived. Aunt Zahava pulled me firmly along, turning to look me up and down between sentences.

"I thought you'd never come! We've been waiting an hour. They said the landing would be late, and I thought to myself, She must be so exhausted!"

Outside, the heat clamped down on me like a metal mask. I squinted blindly in the sun. White taxicabs were parked along the curb, the drivers arguing and haggling with irritated passengers. A cab pulled up in front of us. The window rolled down and the driver looked at us sullenly.

"*L'eipha?* Where to?" he asked.

"Yerushalayim," said my aunt.

"*Shishim,*" he demanded flatly. "Sixty shekels."

My aunt looked at him as if he'd grown a second head.

"We could wait," she said to me in a low voice. "There's a line there by the corner." But I sighed, because really, I simply could not wait.

The driver waved impatiently. "*Ya'alah!*" he shouted. "*Acharey zeh l'daber!* Afterward, you'll talk! *Ken uh lo?* Yes or no?"

Aunt Zahava said yes.

The taxi moved slowly out of the terminal, past security gates and sharp-eyed police, and finally sped up on the main road.

"Four years is a long time," my aunt said, and I looked out the window, nodding. She wanted to know how the flight had been.

"Were the stewardesses nice? Was the food all right? Isn't the view beautiful from the plane? Did you manage to sleep at all?"

We chatted about my cousins, the ones I used to play with, all teenagers now. They were in school till late afternoon, so there would be quiet at home and I could rest.

Outside, houses with red tiled roofs flew by, and advertisements in Hebrew for a new and healthier yogurt. A blur of

Hebrew-English signs pointed the way to Telstone, Ramallah, and Jerusalem. It was strange being here again, driving past the half-remembered landscape, colors, smells, and images coming at me as my mind grasped at hazy recollections from long ago. The radio was on. My eyes closed in the lull of the car's motion, and for a moment I dozed off. I could hear the broadcaster reporting the weather, the sharp trill and twirl of the Hebrew *r* and *l* like little curls unfolding from inside his throat. Just then a semitrailer pulled ahead of the taxi, blowing its horn, and I jumped.

My aunt smiled. She observed me fondly. I looked away, embarrassed.

"You need to sleep," she declared. "I can already see. First you will rest, then you'll unpack, and then, when you are ready, you'll go see your brother at Aunt Itta's."

I nodded, yawning.

"So," she said, leaning in as if to share with me a secret. "Are you excited to see your brother?"

"Of course," I said, my head moving up and down mechanically. "I am really excited to see my brother."

The hills of Jerusalem rose about a mile ahead on the road like an ancient drawing on dusty parchment paper. The landscape widened as we came closer, a rare green sprouting out of the desert brown, hills growing, mound upon mound, a city rising and bending along their curves, clinging to their age-old slopes.

Aunt Zahava wanted to know if I remembered the Welcome to Jerusalem sign, its carved white letters set into the hill at the entrance to the city, but I did not. She wanted to know if the medieval-looking tower to the left of the intersection a few blocks into the city was familiar, but it was not. There was so much I could not recall from when I was last here, the summer before second grade. We drove up Ben-Gurion Boulevard and toward Jaffa Road. At the corner where the Jerusalem Hotel stood, the driver turned abruptly, following my aunt's directions, into the streets of the ultraorthodox neighborhood. He veered impatiently around a passing cab and sped down the narrow, winding streets, which were barely wide enough for one car. In the trunk, my luggage jostled and thumped against the backs of our seats.

At last the taxi stopped. A short, stout building stared down at me from the corner, its once white stones worn beige, the blinds in the windows pulled down to keep out the noonday sun. The last time I was here, the three-story building had loomed at least ten floors high and a mile wide.

After unloading my suitcases, I stood on the stone floor in Aunt Zahava's apartment, staring at the portraits of rebbes hanging neatly on the walls. The memories came back to me now, wrapped in the heavy scent of Sano detergent, used in every Israeli home. The warm smell of coffee crumb cake followed, wafting out of the kitchen, and with it the time I had hidden under the table an hour past bedtime, scooping up the crumbs that had fallen onto the floor.

In the kitchen, my aunt pulled the cake out of the oven. She laughed, watching me down two cups of cold milk and three slices of cake, as she talked about the days when I was *this small*. Then she took me to my cousins' room, clucking worriedly around me as I lay down on the narrow mattress.

"Now you must rest," she commanded, plugging the table fan into the wall socket. "Then you will unpack. And only then, when you feel like a new person, you will go to your brother."

She closed the door behind her, and I turned, facing the fan. But it was useless in this heat, the waves of stifling air blowing this way and that. I was tired and uncomfortable, unbearably hot, and no matter which way I rolled, I could not fall asleep.

I wanted to go home now. My relief at being off the plane was already gone. I wanted badly to board the first aircraft they would let me on, and head straight back to New York.

Was a minute long enough to see my brother? Would it suffice for a hello and good-bye if I promised to return in another six years? From my Aunt Itta's, I'd take a taxi to Tel Aviv, and the first available seat to JFK airport. From there I'd take a cab to Borough Park, and from Borough Park a bus to the Catskills, to the lush green grass and warm breezes rushing through the trees in the colony. In the evenings, I'd sit outside, chatting with my friends, and if the weather was right, during the long afternoons we'd row out onto the lake in the old canoes. I'd stay there happily all day, every day, for sixty mornings and just as many evenings of the summer, the way I'd always done.

I stared listlessly at the bookshelves above the bed, full of books written in Hebrew. I was so far away from home.

Thirty-Seven

In the fall of 1991, when I was in sixth grade, a book called *My Special Brother* was published. The book was the first of its kind among religious Jews. It told the true story of a woman and her younger brother, who had Down syndrome and whom her mother had decided to keep when he was a baby.

At Chava Dushinsky's wedding, between the first and second courses, Blimi's aunt, Mrs. Weinberg, said that the book had made her cry. She shook her head and sighed, choosing the flounder over the salmon, and called the book a must-read, an absolute must-read for everyone in the community. Mrs. Epstein had nodded, agreeing. She said the crispy fried flounder was absolutely delicious. And that she had read *My Special Brother* too, and that, truly, it was heartbreaking, so difficult to understand this negative attitude toward "special" children when it was so perfectly clear that they carried higher souls.

Mrs. Weinberg went on to say that schools were putting the book in their libraries, and that Eichler's Judaica store had built a tower of copies by the window. The last time she'd passed by, they were all gone, sold out.

Mrs. Cohn nodded, impressed. She said, "Yes, I know the family. The mother is such a special person. Just amazing. *Loh Aleinu, nebech.* God forbid the Lord should bring such tragedies on us."

My mother did not hear this conversation. She was seated at the far end of the wedding hall near Ruchela and Leah's mother. I could see the back of her red wig bobbing up and down as she conversed with the others around her table.

I sat at the girls' table, now empty of girls, watching my friends dance with the bride in the center circle. Our table, where the younger, unmarried cousins were seated, was next to the one where Blimi's aunt was chatting with her friends. But Mrs. Epstein never realized that I could hear her; Mrs. Weinberg never noticed that I was there, that I could see her angry expression as she dropped her fork with a sharp clang and stood up. This happened during the third course, after the waiters had brought out stuffed chicken and apple strudel. Mrs. Weinberg had been speaking of her close friends, the Kleins, and their latest *shidduch,* to the Sternbachs.

"The rich ones," she said. "From London. They'll pay for everything, of course. Who would believe the girl is already eighteen and ready for marriage? Why, it was just yesterday that she was born . . ."

Mrs. Borenstein, the shul matchmaker, who had just joined the table, said yes, it really was, and whatever happened with the *shidduch* that had been suggested for Ruchy, Mrs. Weinberg's daughter—that boy from that family in Belgium?

Mrs. Weinberg said, eh, she wasn't sure. She had heard great things about them, but Belgium was far away, and they were looking for a family that could pay, though of course it wasn't completely off the table. After all, she'd heard that the boy was brilliant . . .

Mrs. Borenstein said, "Ah, but he is. Truly brilliant." And that Mrs. Weinberg should strongly consider such a well-respected . family, perfect in every way except for their youngest—a special child, but very high-functioning, so still worth a serious look. She smiled across the table at Mrs. Weinberg, her eager eyes like two lightbulbs.

But Blimi's aunt had not known that there was any special child. The matchmaker who made the suggestion had never said a word about a *special child*. Mrs. Weinberg dropped the fork she'd been holding and pushed back her chair, a withering look on her face. She stood tall and firm on all three inches of heel, the hem of her modest skirt flapping against her mid-calf.

"How dare you!" she said to Mrs. Borenstein. "Would *you* take such a *shidduch* for *your* daughter?"

And furthermore, she said, just because they were not the richest family, and just because her husband was no great rabbi or scholar, and just because her oldest daughter, Ruchy, was not at the very top of her class, certainly did not mean that they deserved a broken match. Her oldest daughter, Ruchy, was a fine and pious girl with good character and a heart of gold. In fact, in the twelfth grade she had won the Chessed and Good Deeds Award, logging by far the most hours of community service for helping the old ladies in the Scharome Manor nursing home off Ocean Parkway.

Mrs. Borenstein tried to explain. She said that the Baums' problem child was only a small problem, a partly higher soul, nothing really "special" like very Down syndrome, *loh Aleinu, loh Aleinu,* the Lord should not bring tragedies on us. But Mrs. Weinberg had already moved to another table.

Mrs. Epstein patted the matchmaker, nodding uncomfortably along. Mrs. Cohn looked as though she had swallowed a sour trout. The matchmaker sighed. Still, it was a powerful book, they all said. One that made you cry.

I hadn't read the book, and had no intention of ever doing so.

Thirty-Eight

The directions to Aunt Itta's apartment were simple: straight up the hill and back down the other side. Follow the road to your left until you hit the bottom at Rabbi Yehuda Street. It was building number three, the fourth floor.

I waved good-bye to my aunt, who was shouting down instructions from the second floor, and started slowly up the hill, passing the grocery where Chayala and I had bought milk for her mother and where we'd seen the hell-going soldier. I laughed to myself as I sipped ice-cold water from the bottle my aunt had given me, switching on the tiny handheld fan for relief.

Before leaving my aunt's apartment, I had wanted to ask her a few questions, about Nachum and the changes in him— whether any of it was true. Because I was scared that my mother had lied, that my Aunt Itta had backed up her story out of pity and kindness, and that the image of Nachum in my mother's mind was a delusion, a mirage created by desperate hope.

It was like that with special children. I had seen it happen—
mothers believing what others said only out of pity. It was that
way in the bungalow colony a few summers back, when some
teenage girls had complimented Mrs. Leiber about her two-
year-old Down syndrome son. They had looked at him, smiles
stretched wide across their faces, eyes oozing sincerity.

"Oh, he's so *cute! * He speaks *very* clearly for such a child.
It's *amazing* what he can do," they said.

When every word a child speaks is a miracle, it does not say
much about real change.

So I hadn't asked my aunt about my brother. Maybe I was
scared that she, too, would lie to me. And if she wouldn't,
then did I really want to hear the truth?

I passed the intersection at the top of the hill, and the large
building that housed the Tnuva dairy factory. Enormous steel
silos loomed up over the gates. I could see a worker, like a
miniature plaything, climbing the ladder on its side. To my left,
the road meandered down Geulah Street and its bustling shops
and kiosks. To my right, the avenue split into a four-lane road,
traffic crawling past a long row of old apartment buildings.

A city bus drove by just then, its tires squealing and grind-
ing to an abrupt halt, the driver shouting at passengers,
"Achorah! Achorah! To the back!"

Not far from where I stood, about a half hour's walk away,
was Jerusalem's central train station, the one Nachum had
gone searching for when he was eight years old.

A short, grizzled man shoved a bouquet of wilting roses in my face. "Five shekel!" he shouted. "Only five shekel! Practically free!" An elderly, sharp-faced woman pushed by him, ordering him to stop and leave the girl alone. Did he not see that no one wanted his wilting flowers? Quickly, I walked away, down the hill.

Thirty-Nine

My mother had learned of Nachum's disappearance weeks after it happened. Savtah Miriam, in New York for Passover, had looked out the car window on the way from JFK airport and said, "How are you going to drive in such weather? This is what the rain was like the day Nachum ran away—"

Aunt Chana, sitting in the back, had pinched my grandmother hard, but my mother had already heard. Savtah Miriam promised her that nothing had happened, really nothing, but my mother pulled the car to the side of the road. She took the key out of the ignition.

"This car will not move," she said very quietly, "until I know what happened to my son."

"Oh, it was nothing, really nothing," my grandmother had nervously said. Though maybe just a small something. Shortly after my mother had left Nachum in Israel, no one could find the boy for five terrifying hours. It was as if he'd disappeared from the face of the earth.

In the end, my grandmother was forced to explain about that afternoon when, somehow, the staff at the school for children with special needs had not noticed that there was one fewer child on the van going home. Somehow the monitoring teacher had closed the door of the vehicle and told the driver that it was time to go—already they were off schedule.

Inside the building, my brother had waited patiently. He had waited for the silence to settle in, for the sounds of ticking clock hands to echo in the empty corridors, telling him that everyone was gone. Then, cautiously, he opened the door of the supply closet and stepped out. Quickly, he left the building and began to run.

Aunt Itta had stood outside on Rabbi Yehuda Street the way she did every day, waiting for the school van to come. But when the door opened, the assistant teacher facing her looked pale and scared.

"Nachum is not in the van," she said. "I checked three times, under every seat. I checked behind the—"

Aunt Itta, fear rising in her throat, said, "What do you mean, *he's not in the van? Where is the child?*"

On the steps going up to the fourth floor, Aunt Itta had shouted at her daughters to come down, now! Nachum was gone. He had never gotten in the van.

The pale teacher could not explain how it had happened. She drove back to the school with Ayalah and Batya. Aunt Itta called Uncle Zev from where he was studying at the

synagogue. The teacher called the principal as the girls
searched the building. They searched the classrooms, the cel-
lar, and behind a pile of desks; they searched the storage
room, the school yard, and the empty supply closet. They
called Nachum's name softly, then loudly, pleading for him to
come out.

Someone called the police.

"We have never had such an incident before," said the grim-
faced principal to the men in blue uniforms. "This child is a
problem—no teacher can control him. Our children are always accounted for."

Ayalah and Batya stood outside, wondering which way
to look first. The rain pounded against their umbrellas and
gusts of wind swirled angrily. It rarely ever rained this way in
Jerusalem.

On the other side of the city, Nachum walked, his wool
jacket wrapped around him like a cold, wet sponge. For
blocks on end he had run, past familiar buildings and synagogues, past supermarkets and bus stops, until he no longer
recognized the streets around him, the empty corners and
shuttered stores.

Somewhere past the center of the city, he stopped. Maybe
he was too cold; maybe in the pouring rain he had lost his
hawklike sense of direction, which had been pointing him toward the central train station. Maybe it was the large puddle
he saw, like a tiny pond in the middle of the road, behind

a corner kiosk. Nachum looked down at the puddle, at the plunking, pattering drops falling in it. Then he began to jump.

In the dimly lit kiosk, a man with walnut-colored skin and a Star of David necklace pulled down the shutters. Not since Noah's flood had rain come down like this. There was not a mortal soul in sight, no business to wait for—not in this weather. The man came out the side door. He opened his umbrella, but the thrashing wind blew it right out of his hand, turned it inside out, and sent it spinning across the street. The man cursed. Stepping out, he pulled up the zipper of his jacket, the hood over his head, and ran.

But then he stopped, one foot in the street, one still on the curb. He turned, shielding his eyes from the rain, and stepped closer, a bit closer, just to see if there really was a boy there, a lone young boy, jumping in a puddle behind his shuttered kiosk.

On the boy's head was a drenched *kippa;* dark side curls stuck to his cheeks. Streams of water poured from his wool jacket and from the tzitzit strings hanging from his pants. The boy was perhaps seven or eight. The nearest religious neighborhood was miles away.

The man called out to the boy.

"*Yeled!* Little boy! *Eiphah Ima?* Where is your mother?"

But the boy who looked up at him did not speak, could not tell him that he was in fact looking for his mother. He went back to jumping.

The man bent closer, trying to find the boy's eyes. "*Mah atah oseh pah l'vad?* What are you doing here? Why are you alone?"

But the boy did not look up again. He looked only at the puddle as he jumped up and down, splashing, splashing in the rain.

At the local police station on Rachalvi Street, Uncle Zev sat, white as a ghost. He watched the men standing around murmuring as an officer mapped out the city streets. An hour earlier, Uncle Zev had called a neighbor, who had called his cousin, who had called the neighbors and the men from the shul.

The child had been gone for nearly three hours. The rain would not let up. The police dogs could not follow a scent in such weather. The rain could go on all night this way, but they could not wait for it to stop. They needed to search now.

The officer pointed at the map. If the boy went west, he would reach the highway. If he went east, he would reach the old city and its Arab neighborhoods. The checkpoints and surrounding police stations had been notified, soldiers alerted at the borders. All vehicles were to be checked for a child, age eight, who did not speak.

The rain came down in sheets, curtains of water sweeping across the city. It was as if a dam had broken in the sky above, said the men. Not since Noah had there been such rain.

Behind the shuttered kiosk, a mile or two away, Nachum stopped jumping.

He stood in the puddle, shivering, and stared, mesmerized, at the plunking raindrops in the pond, tiny rippling circles, widening in ringlike patterns. He did not face the hooded man, nor the second one, who had joined him. He could see their mouths moving, making urgent sounds. Their hands gestured toward him; scared, he stepped back. They moved away. My brother waited. Then, as they watched, he jumped in and out, in and out of the puddle again.

The men would not leave. Sometimes they looked around the corner, as if expecting someone to come. They murmured worriedly with each other. Surely there must be a parent, a babysitter, an older sibling—somebody—searching for this child.

From down the block a car approached. A man wearing a small knitted *kippa* peered out through the windshield. The car slowed down, the driver looking curiously, then suspiciously, at the two bareheaded Middle Eastern men standing over a shivering boy with side curls who squinted back at him in the glare of the headlights.

Fear flashed through his mind. *Arabs,* he thought. *Arabs!* No child with a *kippa* wandered these streets. And he slammed on the brakes and jumped out, striding up to the curb.

"What's going on here?" he demanded. Then, finally noticing one man's Star of David pendant, he lowered his voice, relieved. "What's happening?" he asked. "What are you doing with the boy?"

The men stared at him, confused. "We don't know," the hooded one said. "I found him here, outside my kiosk, jumping in the puddle. The boy does not speak—he does not answer any questions. It's like he doesn't see us at all. We've been standing here for half an hour. He won't budge from the puddle."

The man in the knitted *kippa* bent down, his hands gentle on Nachum's trembling arms. The boy was ice-cold, his lips quivering blue, his fists clenched against the sides of his jacket.

"*Yeled,*" the man said. "*Boh.* Come inside the car. It's warm in there. I will drive you back home."

The man pushed the boy gently forward, one hand on each shoulder. Maybe Nachum was too tired, maybe he realized he would not reach the trains that day, and that's why he followed the man. He left the puddle and got into the car.

The man in the *kippa* told the others that he'd take the boy back home. Then he pulled off the boy's jacket, his shoes, and his frigid socks. He wiped off his face and hands with a paper towel, turning the heat on the highest setting. Gently, he asked the boy for his name, and if he knew where he lived.

But the boy did not speak. He stared at the windshield wipers, his eyes transfixed by the blades swinging right to left, right to left. The boy did not seem to hear, to know where he'd come from, or where it was he planned to go. It was as if the rain had dropped him from the sky.

The man drove west, to the religious neighborhoods where the ultraorthodox lived. He circled block after block, went up one hill and down another. Perhaps the child would point or show a glimmer of recognition upon seeing a building he knew. In the seat to the man's right, the boy gazed out the window, looking, looking for the lost trains.

It was dark outside, and much time had passed since he'd found Nachum standing in the puddle, when the man pulled up at the first police station. Holding the boy's hand, he took him inside and sat him down. He woke the police officer dozing at his desk, and told him what had happened. The officer picked up the phone and dialed the surrounding stations. He told them that the lost boy was here, brought in by a man in a knitted *kippa*.

And this is how the story came to an end. Hours after he'd disappeared from the supply closet in the school that was not for autistic children, my brother was brought home in the cold rain by Uncle Zev and some men from shul. Aunt Itta wrapped him up in dry pajamas and warm towels, all the while weeping in relief.

It took days for Aunt Itta to understand why Nachum had run away and what he had been looking for. Maybe it was through picture cards, or the objects he meticulously drew. Maybe it was the broken sounds he made that explained that at the central station there were many trains. The trains rode out on steel tracks to different, faraway places. There was the train that took people to Haifa, to Tel Aviv, and to the shores of Eilat. Nachum was looking for the train that took people to America, to New York. On the train, he'd hide in the luggage compartment or under the seats. Then he'd wait for the train to reach the stop across the sea, to take him back home to his mother in New York.

*   *   *

Several months after Nachum ran away, he was diagnosed with autism. Six months or so after that, he was finally transferred to Jerusalem's only school for autistic children.

When the principal told my mother that the school was not very Orthodox, my mother laughed. When the principal told her that ultraorthodox families refused to send their children there, no matter how severe their issues were, my mother cried. She said, "You worry about my son's autism. Let God worry for his religion."

In the summer of 1991, Nachum began attending the Jerusalem school. And the story began to change.

Forty

The number on the building said eight, though from far away it looked like a three or a five. It was hard to be sure in the blinding sun. Five more buildings to go. I folded up my sleeve and gulped down the last of the water, dropping the minifan in a nearby trash can. Stupid gadget broke just when I needed it most.

A man walked past me dressed in Chassidic garb: a large black *kippa* on his head, closed leather shoes on his feet. The ends of his pant legs were tucked into a pair of black socks pulled over his calves to his knees. Perhaps he knew how much farther till the bottom of the hill and if I'd reach it before I died. But the man walked ahead, side curls swinging briskly as if it was a fine day to wear an overcoat and socks. I trudged along, hands shading my eyes, trying to hide from the sun.

The number on the building said three, and I looked up, trying to remember it. It looked the same as the others, five floors high, once white stones covered with grime, narrow porches jutting randomly about. Between the iron rods of the porches, children's toys cheerfully looked out over the street.

High above me, a young woman leaned from a window, and I thought I saw a knowing smile on her face. She waved at me, her dark curls bouncing. I could hear her laugh as she straightened up, disappearing back in through the window. Abruptly, my stomach churned. I looked up the hill I'd come down. I could still run.

I forced myself up the stone steps and into the shady passageway. Breathless, I leaned against the cool stone wall. To my right were the mailbox units, to my left a bulletin board with notices tacked on. Across the corridor, a wrought-iron stairwell spiraled up to the fourth floor. This was where my brother lived.

A door swung open, its hinges squealing. I heard voices somewhere above me. Hebrew words bounced off the corridor walls. I stood still, one foot on the staircase, the other on the welcome mat, and took a deep breath.

Then I ran up without stopping. If I stopped, I knew my legs would not go up again. Just two more flights of stairs, and they'd be there, the family I barely remembered. I tucked in my shirt nervously. I would not turn around now and flee from this place, not until I saw my brother.

I jumped over the last two steps and paused. Aunt Itta stood at the open door, her arms spread out in welcome. To her right I could see my cousins Ayalah and Batya grinning widely, to her left a fleeting shadow on the apartment wall. Then I was pulled into their smothering embraces and I could see no more.

Aunt Itta stepped back and took my chin in her hand.

"You look just the same," she exclaimed, "except now you're as tall as I am!"

Ayalah laughed. "Your smile hasn't changed one bit," she chimed. "You still have that one cute dimple."

Batya hugged me tightly, smiling happily.

I remembered my cousins now, their dark, bouncy hair, Batya's open, friendly face, just as it was the summer before second grade. I remembered my aunt now, her chin-length wig and warm brown eyes glimmering through the frames of her outdated glasses.

She stroked my arm and asked me questions, but I was too overwhelmed to hear them. Then she and my cousins led me inside.

Batya sat me down on the couch in the living room. Ayalah put a glass in my hand. Someone asked if I wanted kiwi juice, fruit punch, or water. I said kiwi. No, fruit punch. No, water, please.

Batya stood at the threshold of the room, calling out, "Nachum! Nachum, *boh. Boh enah.* Come now. Your sister is waiting to see you!"

It was as if the room had stood still for six years, waiting. It was as though the apartment had been set up all over again, every serving plate and cup in the same place as the last time I was here. The beige stone tiles that we'd played on, the sliding doors that we'd ridden on, the leafy houseplants still in the sunniest corner. Overlooking the hills were the windows where I had waited for the breeze to come in. There were the picture frames on the small corner table in front of which Ayalah had braided my hair. There was the bookcase stacked up to the ceiling, sagging beneath the weight of a hundred holy books.

Uncle Zev walked into the room right then, a holy book in his hand. He smiled at me and asked me how the flight had been. Then he sat down to read in his familiar mahogany chair at the head of the rosewood table. The table was covered with an embroidered white tablecloth, the one reserved for the Sabbath, holidays, and guests. Behind my uncle, in the small china cabinet, stood the silver kiddush cups and menorah, just the way I remembered. And there was the corner where I had watched my brother playing alone the day we left six years ago.

I looked at the glass in my hand filled with fruit juice. On my lap was a plate of strawberries and sponge cake. I nibbled at the edge of the slice of cake.

"Where's Nachum?" I asked.

"He's in his room," Ayalah answered. "He hid there as soon as he heard you on the stairs. Don't worry. He'll come out. He needs some time."

I smiled, uncertain. Batya explained, "He's shy!" She smiled reassuringly. "Nachum's been up since dawn, waiting. He was so excited, he could not sit still for a minute. He's been coming and going from the window all morning."

I munched silently on the cake, not sure what to say. But then Batya asked me if I still had the erasers she'd given me the last time, just before I left.

"Yes," I said, relieved to talk about something else. "That is, Rivky still has them. She took them from me as soon as we got back to New York. She promised me she'd save them in her collection for the day I got married. She told me the erasers would be worth a lot of money then. So I haven't seen them since second grade."

Batya laughed. She said that she had more erasers for me. As many as I wanted.

"Well," I said, "how much are they worth?"

"Very little, I'm afraid," she said.

I giggled awkwardly. Then Batya asked me if I still liked *petel*, a syrupy fruit punch popular in Israeli homes. Back then it had been my favorite drink. I laughed and said I wasn't sure. I would have to taste it again.

My cousins sat down, one on each side of me. From the corner cabinet beneath the holy books, Batya had brought piles of stencils in geometric shapes. She pulled scissors from a plastic container and held them out to Ayalah, who rolled her eyes. Ayalah asked if I wanted to help.

"Batya's a kindergarten teacher, the best one in the city. But the work she has every day... Look, seventeen doll faces to cut out, then seventeen doll skirts. And then thirty-four doll shoes." She looked at me, teasing. "You see, if you don't help, I'll have to do it, and if I see one more piece of paper to cut and paste, I'll scream. Please?"

Batya glowered at her sister.

"Ayalah!" she exclaimed. "The girl just walked off the plane. Lazy is what you are, that's all." Then she held out the scissors to her sister again.

Ayalah took the scissors and clipped them mockingly in the air. She asked me if summer camp was really all that fun. And what in heaven's name did we *do* there for eight weeks?

I pulled another pair of scissors from the container, though Batya insisted that I shouldn't. I shrugged and said it was okay. I didn't have anything else to do. Then I carefully cut along the dotted lines as I told my cousins about summer camp.

Somewhere in the middle of our conversation, Aunt Itta walked in holding a plate of cookies, the phone between her shoulder and ear. She pointed to the receiver, winking at me, as she loudly reassured Aunt Zahava that there was no need to worry. I had arrived at the apartment safe and sound, in one whole piece, and yes, I was a carbon copy of my mother. She then placed the cookies on the table and walked back out, still chatting.

Batya said that she thought I was a very brave girl. She'd never manage to be away from home for eight weeks. Ayalah said that I'd always been brave, even as a child.

"Do you remember the kibbutz farm we visited?" she asked. "How you ran away from the angry goat, after you tried stuffing a whole potato into its mouth—three times!"

I did not remember. Batya did, and she doubled over, giggling.

"Oh, you were such a funny kid," she said. "A trouble-maker." She patted my arm affectionately and asked me if I wanted to come with her the next morning to the kindergarten where she taught. If I was bored, I could make arts and crafts from her supply closet.

"It'll be fun," she said, filling my plate with more strawberries. "You could even help me with the kids, if you'd like."

I leaned back and stretched out my arms. I told Batya that I wasn't sure. Kindergarten sounded like fun, but I'd rather go to the Western Wall. Or to the open-air market in the main square. Or to the windmill in the old city. Or anywhere else but kindergarten.

Batya said I was still a character. I tried to answer, but my jaws opened into an endless yawn. Then another and another. It was as if my exhausted brain had decided to shut down. I could not keep my eyes open.

Ayalah said I must lie down and rest. She brought a pillow to the couch so I could nap comfortably. "When you wake up, you'll feel refreshed. After you sleep a bit."

Batya said that my eyes were red from exhaustion. She said she'd see to it that I didn't sleep for long. This way my body would adapt to the local time. And Aunt Itta, standing behind the couch, said something about meringues. There was a batch in the oven, I thought I heard her say.

I wanted to tell my aunt that I loved meringues, but my mouth would no longer articulate my thoughts. Sugar and egg whites, mixed, stirred, and twisted into Hershey's Kiss–shaped puffs of cloud. I remembered the last one I'd had, crusty on the outside, gooey on the inside—paradise melting in the mouth. It was the only one left in the bag that Aunt Itta had given my mother: two for each child, for the plane ride home.

But I'd eaten all twelve meringues, from first to last. I hadn't left even one for my siblings. It wasn't my fault that they'd slept through most of the flight, along with my mother. They could have stayed up like me, and watched the in-flight Disney movie, sneaking meringue after meringue from the bag.

I opened my eyes. Holy books peered righteously down at me from a bookshelf. Wooden chairs sat, empty, around the table. It was silent in the living room where I'd dozed off. In the rooms around me, voices murmured quietly and I sighed, my mind absorbing the stillness. When had I fallen asleep? What had awakened me? Wait—was I still in Israel?

A voice was leaving the kitchen, moving closer, growing louder as it came into the room. Then it stopped. I shifted but did not sit up. I was still too tired to move. Head on the pillow, I looked up, searching the space behind me. From over the armrest I could see my cousin Batya. She stood in the doorway, her mouth open in midsentence, looking toward the corner of the room.

My eyes followed hers across the room, to the space between the green plants and the couch, where a boy stood, his green eyes boring into mine. My mind jolted to a stop. I recognized him by the dimples that appeared when he smiled. Abruptly, I sat up.

Four years had passed since I'd last seen Nachum, the boy who had tumbled out of the sky. Four years had passed since I'd heard him, a boy imprisoned in the labyrinth of his broken mind. I remembered this brother, his sealed-up face and inward-looking eyes. I remembered his lips, like two painted lines, and a mouth with no tongue inside to speak. I remembered the boy because he'd been a patched-together thing, made of disconnected pieces, a child struck by an angel, once for the Torah, once for his speech, and once for the rest of his mind.

"Nachum is different now," my mother had said, and I had pretended to believe.

"You won't recognize him," she had told me proudly, and I had listened as if to some faraway legend about a crazy boy.

But I never knew just how much of my brother had been stolen until the moment I saw him that day, and it was as if the angels had given it all back. When he looked at me, in his eyes there was light, and on his lips there was a smile. When he spoke, in the sounds there was meaning, word touching word, thoughts connecting in the mind.

"Meh-nuchah? Meh-nuchah?...Meh-nuchah?" In his voice I heard wonder. "You, you, you—you are my sister, Meh-nuchah."

This was not the boy I had known.

This boy was taller and broader than I was. This boy sat down close to me on the couch. This boy laid his hand cautiously over mine, repeating, "Meh-nuchah, Meh-nuchah," as if getting used to the sound of my name.

"Meh-nuchah? Meh...Meh...Meh-nuchah. You are my sister, Meh-nuchah. Today...today...today...you are my sister."

This boy stroked my fingers, very gently. He gazed intently into my face, searching, because what if I was really just a fleeting idea? It was as if, in his mind, I was not yet firm enough, my existence still uncertain. If he looked away at the wrong moment, I might disappear—forever this time.

"You. You are my sister. Sis—sis—sister. You, you, you—you are my sister."

"Yes," I said. "I am your sister."

Aunt Itta stood silently by, Uncle Zev next to her, the holy book closed in his hand. Ayalah stood at the threshold, her hand on Batya's shoulder, on both of their faces a startled smile. They watched us, this family I barely knew, as though the words between Nachum and me held the power of a sacred prayer.

I let my brother hold my hand, feel my fingers, and call my name. Because on such a day, I knew, seeing wasn't enough. Touch was needed, and sound too, every sense summoned to secure a place in his world for this new and sudden sister. For four years I'd been gone, stored in the back rooms of a distant past, an array of broken bits and pieces. And now I was here, all at once, and in his mind I was connecting, bit by bit, part by part, like the final pieces of a puzzle.

"Meh-nuchah? Y-y-y-you. You are my sis—sister."

Ayalah giggled, I don't know why. From my lungs, my breath came up sharply and I realized I'd been holding it this whole time. I breathed in slowly now, in and out again. Then I reached down under the couch and pulled out the bag from my mother. I gave it to Nachum.

"Hineh ha'mamtakim," I said. "Here are the sweets, Nachum. From America. Everything you like."

He took the bag from my hand without ever moving his eyes from me.

We sat on the couch for a long time. I did not say much, only smiled and agreed that it was true what he said. Today, I was his sister. I was his sister, older by thirteen months. Today, I was his sister, Meh-nuchah. And he, my brother, Nachum.

Forty-One

In Nachum's room there was a closet filled with sweaters, folded neatly into piles and stuffed onto the shelves. Nachum stood by the closet and its half-open door, his eyes carefully following mine. I looked around.

It was a simple room, a high riser bed beneath a curtained window, a birchwood wardrobe set against the opposite wall, a narrow desk tucked into the small space in the corner. Between the desk and the bed frame stood an uneven tower of boxes, some still wrapped up in gift paper.

Through the walls of Nachum's bedroom I could hear my cousins talking in the living room. Aunt Itta had suggested that Nachum show me the apartment, to remind me what their home looked like. My brother had sat up abruptly at the thought, a flash of wonder filling his face, as if he'd just been chosen to lead an important expedition. I dutifully followed him through the doorway to the small central hall, the eyes of our family watching us go.

Nachum showed me the kitchen, the porch, the bedrooms belonging to my aunt and uncle, and my cousins, and finally his own. I sat on his bed and looked up at the circular, fluorescent light fixture on the ceiling. Then I looked at him, watching him struggle for words.

My brother opened his mouth. He closed it. Then he opened it, and closed it again. I could see his mind reaching to gather the words, building a sentence the way he built Lego, searching for the right color and size, his mouth on hold until the sounds formed a pattern, until the shapes were lined up in correct sequence and order. Then the words came out, breathlessly.

"This—this—this—*this* is my room. This—this—*this* is my bed. And—and—and. This is my. This is my room. This is where I sleep."

He observed me sitting on his bed, my hand stroking his linen-covered pillow. He leaned forward but then halted, straightening up. He hesitated, as if still trying to find his way around new terrain: someone touching his pillow. I moved my hand off the bed.

He said again, "This—this—this is my room. You... you...you...but you could sit on my bed. My...my...my pih—pillow. I—I—I don't mind. Meh-Menuchah."

I nodded, half standing, and then quickly sat back down.

"Thank you," I said. I looked around. I could feel the silence. I pointed to the wall behind him, where a multicolored laminated chart hung, each square illustrated with the picture of a different task or chore.

"What's that?" I asked. "What is that sign? Did you get it from school?"

Nachum turned, as if the chart had appeared right then. His eyes absorbed the words, the lines, and the small figures. Then he said yes—yes—yih-yes, it was a chart from his teacher at school. For the mornings. To remember things to be done. Like washing hands. Like brushing teeth. Like saying the morning blessing, and tying his shih—shih—shih—shoes. At the end of the week, there was a reward. Something he liked. Chips, or ice cream.

I nodded. Nachum looked at me, his eyebrows furrowed in concentration. His eyes searched the room, as if seeking the elusive thing that would tell him what came now, what it was he must do. I waited, watching his eyes bore into the floor.

Finally, he looked up, his shoulders easing. He walked to the wardrobe along the wall. He sat down in front of it, folded his legs comfortably, and pulled out a bottom drawer. I watched my brother, his back hunched and hands rummaging eagerly through electronic gadgets my mother had sent. He looked up, waving a camera.

"Yih—yih—y-you. You want to see my cam-ihra? My... cam-ihra?"

"Yes," I said. I most certainly wanted to see his camera.

I got off the bed and sat down next to him, beneath a knitted sleeve dangling off an upper shelf. The sleeve swung limply above our heads, swaying in the afternoon breeze.

I remembered the knitted pullover and its sky-blue sleeves; I remembered the shirts and vests my mother had purchased in the children's section of Macy's. I had tagged along behind her, whining and complaining, watching her skip over sale racks and sift instead through the new arrivals—pants, turtle-necks, expensive sweaters—without a second thought.

I had chosen a dress for myself, one that had three silk roses and a white leather belt, but my mother said no. There had been a petticoat beneath the skirt, and pink flowers along the hem, but my mother had taken the dress from my hand and firmly placed it back on the rack. Oh, she'd buy me a dress for the holiday, she said, but I should look only at the sale rack.

Because for me, hand-me-downs were good enough—the well-worn, faded clothes from my fat older sister. More than once, I'd been forced to throw an ugly old dress of Rivky's clear across a room before my mother agreed that, though it was unnecessary, she'd buy me something new.

And it wasn't just me who suffered. My mother bought clothes on sale for all five of us, three girls and my two other brothers. But she shopped for Nachum, the faraway child, separately. For him she bought cashmere for winter and fine knits for summer. For him she bought shirts made in Italy and France. She'd pack them neatly in her suitcase—price tags ripped off and discarded. This was no cast-off boy.

Sometimes I helped carry the bags from the bedroom to the dining room table; they held boxes of sweets, gifts tied up in ribbons, piles of games and colorful toys. These would be tucked into the corners of suitcases already filled with new sweaters and shoes. The Mary Poppins bag, I called it, bottomless and endless, filled to the brim with sweets and nice things—tokens for my brother of my mother's love.

*　　*　　*

"Meh-nuchah? Meh-nuchah—look."

Nachum held up a camera. He pointed to a small button, showing me how it worked. Then he pulled out a packet of pictures he'd taken of birds in a park. He held out a disc player my mother had bought him for music, and another one, a sleeker kind, that she'd sent just a few months before.

The drawer was bursting with the things that had been sent from across the ocean: two cameras, three watches— one with a hidden audio recorder, another glow-in-the-dark. There was the waterproof camera that Nachum rarely used, and professional-grade binoculars—"*Kih-kih-kih—k'moh ba-tzavah*. Lih-lih-lih-like in the army. Th-th-th—*that* shows things cih-learly. Very cih-learly. Even. Even in the dark."

So this was where the gifts and the clothes settled down, the closet and room where they were unpacked. Here was the home of the boy who had been hovering in the background, just around the corner of our lives.

Uncle Zev called out from the entrance hall, his voice beckoning my brother. "Nachum, *boh*," he said. "Nachum, come. In only five minutes, it's mincha."

Quickly, my brother stood up. I looked at him curiously. "Do you go to afternoon prayers every day?" I asked.

"Yih-yih-yes," he said. "Ev-ihry day I go. To pray."

He stared at me intently, as if decoding the words my eyes said.

"M-maybe, ah…and maybe—I could walk you to Aunt Z'ava. After prayers."

"Maybe," I said, "if Aunt Itta agrees, you will walk me back."

I followed Nachum to the foyer, where Uncle Zev stood, pulling on his suit jacket and hat. He smiled, watching us approach, pride spreading out like gentle ripples from the corners of his eyes and over his face.

From the kitchen, Aunt Itta gestured at me to come. Nachum went to find his sweater as I asked my aunt about waiting for Nachum to walk me back after prayers.

She smiled but shook her head.

"Tell Nachum that you need to leave now," she said in a hush. Ayalah and Batya nodded in agreement.

"It's too much for him at once," Ayalah explained. "He needs to process this slowly, one day at a time. He's seeing you for the first time in years."

Batya patted me on the back. "There's a whole summer ahead," she whispered. "In a week or two, you can spend all your days together. For now, tell him that you must go, but that you'll be back tomorrow at four, when he comes home from school."

They looked at me, waiting for my confirmation, as if I fully understood why things must be this way. I nodded, understanding nothing. Then I went to the hall and told my brother that I needed to leave now after all.

"But tomorrow, at four, I will be here again," I said. "I will come back when you come off the school van…Nachum?"

My brother was pacing the floor anxiously. His eyes blinked

rapidly as he looked up at me, then away, then up at me, and again away. Halting sounds began and stopped in his throat, his voice tangled in knots.

"Ah. Ah. Ah. Ah—so...so...so tomorrow...tomorrow—you will *come?* You will *come?*"

"Yes, Nachum. Tomorrow I will come."

"Ah, ah, ah, at—at four...at four o'clock exactly?"

"At exactly four o'clock, Nachum."

"All, all—all right *then*. Tomorrow—tomorrow I will see you, Meh-nuchah. At four. At four o'clock exactly."

"At four o'clock."

"You will come. You will cih-cih—you will come then."

"I will come then. I promise."

"Tomorrow," he repeated, as if reassuring himself. "To—tomorrow...At four exactly. O'clock."

At the door, he said good-bye.

"You should. You should. You should have...a good night. A vih...a vih-very good night. I will, I will, I will see you...tomorrow. When you come back. My sister."

And he put his arms around me as if to hug me, touching me lightly, then letting go. He picked up my hand, and I wrapped it firmly around his fingers. He looked at me, still unsure, as if I were still only a wishful thought, a new and delicate thing, and if he touched too hard, or talked too loud, I would break, and he wouldn't have a sister anymore.

Part V

Forty-Two

When Nachum first entered the Jerusalem school for autistic children, my Aunt Itta asked the principal a question: What percentage of children graduate from the school?

The principal looked amused. "Zero," she said. "No one graduates from this school. They leave at age twenty, when the program ends."

Three years passed. In June 1992, eleven-year-old Nachum graduated from the school, the first student ever to do so. From there he went to a modern Orthodox junior high school with a resource room. He'd stay on there for the rest of high school, making a network of friends, and with tutors and therapists helping with his special needs.

I remember hearing about all this back home in Brooklyn, hearing my mother describing the miracle that had become of the curse. I remember smiling, nodding along without ever feeling a thing. I had looked at the tears of joy in her eyes, at her pride at my brother's accomplishment, and inside I had shrugged, wondering which role I had gotten in the upcoming school play. The memories came back to me that night, as I sat up, shaken, in my Aunt Zahava's living room. It was silent in the apartment, only the whirling blades of electric fans whispering from every room. My hands cold and clammy, I stared up at the ceiling, at the shadows on the walls.

I had barely escaped the nightmare before it swallowed me alive. In my jet-lagged sleep, I had stood in a small, empty room, waiting for Nachum to come. When he did not, I opened the door and found that I was in a long corridor with many doors on either side. Somehow I knew that I had lost Nachum, that he was in one of the rooms behind those doors, and now I must go and find him.

In the corridor there were people milling about, their faces round blurs. They were faces I knew but could not remember or name. I asked the people if they'd seen my brother Nachum, and they pointed to a nearby door. But when I opened it and stepped inside the room, it was empty. There was only silence.

I turned to leave, but then I saw a boy. He was curled up in the corner, on his knees. A bolt of fear ran through me. This was the wrong boy, rocking, rocking softly. I did not want him to turn around; I desperately did not want him to see me, because I was looking for my other, real brother, not this soundless child.

I quickly left the room and tried another door. I ran through a narrow, winding hallway. "Nachum! Nachum!" I called. Maybe if he heard me, he'd come back, and we could leave this endless place. I turned right, then left, screaming my brother's name. Then I stopped and stumbled backward.

I had nearly tripped on the boy. It was the soundless child, curled in a corner the same way as before, but now he faced right instead of left, rocking harder, his movements more agitated.

I turned and ran again, pushing door after door, searching for Nachum. But it was as if I was trapped inside a maze, and no matter how many doorknobs I turned and rooms I entered, I could not find my brother, only the silent, faceless child. I could hear my voice bouncing off the walls in frightful echoes, growing louder as I ran.

Too late, I noticed that I'd reached the last room in the corridor, and that the rocking boy was now angry. I saw the soundless child fling himself up and back, his body arced in the air like an arrow. Then he lunged forward like a battering ram, his head slamming hard into the wall.

The wall caved in and a dark hole opened up, widening like a gaping mouth. "Nachum! Nachum! Nachum!" I screamed as I ran away, not daring to turn around, but I could feel myself falling, falling. Beneath my feet, the ground gave way to the gaping, angry mouth, and it was swallowing me up. I dropped, screaming, clawing at the vacuum. I knew that I'd lost my brother in the one place I could never find him again.

I woke up. My eyes opened wide, and I heard myself gasp. My jawbone unclenched painfully. I sat up and looked fearfully around. Above me, the moonlit reflections of the crystal chandelier danced across the ceiling.

I could feel my heart pounding in my chest. I was covered in a layer of cold sweat. I threw the sheets off the couch, stumbled to the open window on the other side of the room, and stood there, gulping air.

It was dark outside, the moon dangling from the clouds like an old man's lantern. It was just a dream, just a scary dream that had come because I'd forgotten my nightly prayers. I said this to myself again and again, to my trembling hands and chest, but as I looked up at the stars through the iron window bars, I cried.

On the dresser in my aunt's bedroom that day, I'd seen the fax machine and heard the throb and stir as it awoke. Finally a message glided out, curling over on a roll of silky paper. I could see the words sweeping gracefully across the page, the familiar Hebrew scrawl. It was a letter from my mother in New York.

Near the fax lay a pile of letters curled up and yellowed at the edges like a mound of ancient scrolls. Older letters, I supposed, sent from home in the days and weeks before. And I wondered about the rest of them, the hundreds my mother had written, night after night, year after year, sitting at the kitchen table while the rest of the house was silent and dark. In the background of a thousand dreams, I'd heard the whirring and humming of the machine directing letter after letter overseas.

It was a silklike paper curling out from our own fax in Brooklyn that had told me how much my brother cost. It glided up over the tray one afternoon just as I was searching the desk for a marker. I pulled it out. It was a bill written out in Hebrew for five thousand dollars. Mystified, I'd handed it to my father.

"How much does Nachum cost to fix?" I had asked. "More than regular children?"

My father had laughed. I could not tell whether he thought it was funny, or was just surprised. "Nachum costs ex'ectly like regih'lar children, but six from 'dem toge'der," he said, his tone playful, as if he was telling a joke. "Nachum cuhst like vun whole regih'lar fe'mily."

Horrified, I asked my mother if it was true, my father's maybe-joke about the cost of my brother. Distracted by my sister's strawberry yogurt, just spilled on the floor, and by the balls of gefilte fish she was rolling, my mother answered, as if talking to herself.

"At least as much as a family," she said. The fish balls plunked with a small splash into the bubbling pot. "Sometimes more."

Then she looked up and realized what she'd let slip, the delicate points of a matter never discussed with children. Her eyes flashed with irritation as she looked down at my wide-open mouth and ordered me to close it before my tongue fell right out. She said it was really none of my business how much Nachum, or anyone else, cost. I should never ask again.

For weeks afterward, whenever I remembered what she'd said, a feeling of rage came over me at the enormous sums of money Nachum was taking from our family. If not for him, I knew, we would have already been millionaires.

So one day, when I could no longer restrain myself, I burst out to my father, "But why? Why do you pay so much for an unfixable boy?"

He looked down at me as if I'd just asked an odd question.

"Because he is my boy," he said. And that was that.

It was that mysterious love thing that I thought only my mother carried. But my father had deceived me—he had it too. I suddenly realized that all along it had never really mattered whether he could find Nachum or not; he still wanted my mother to look for him. The boy might drag them round and round in crazy circles, split open the walls, turn everything inside out and upside down, but my father still followed where my mother led. He'd pay forever for my brother because Nachum was his boy.

I shivered in the cool Jerusalem night as I leaned out the open window. There were shadows in the street, like the ones in our yard that evening in third grade, just a few weeks after my mother had brought Nachum home. It had been nearly dark outside when I had peered out the tiny bathroom window, watching my brother in a frenzy of fear hurl himself away from my father. On his hands and knees on the asphalt, my brother spun around like cornered prey trapped between two hunters. My mother reached out, bringing her hands down gently over Nachum's head. She held out her arms, but he pulled away. He crawled frantically from her and into my father's legs.

My mother leaned over Nachum. He stood up, his hands groping at the space around her, and under the night sky, their shadows looked like two great sea creatures writhing and battling.

Then Nachum turned and ran through the yard and out the front gate. My mother ran after him. She caught him and held him as he struggled, his head nearly crashing into the ground. I saw my mother's shadow pulling back, but my brother's shadow was stronger. It pulled on my mother until you could not see what was him and what was her, until it swallowed her whole.

Voices speaking in Hebrew came through the window: my mother crying because my father would not come, my father angry because she would not let go, and Nachum screaming, pulling, pulling, pulling.

But then my father's shadow stirred. He strode toward the gate, his dark form stopping behind my mother's.

"Esther, let him go," he said.

"Let him go?" my mother cried. "Are you crazy?"

"The harder you hold on to him, the more he'll try to run!"

"So what should I do? Throw him to the cars?"

"He won't stop struggling until you let go."

The shadows churned under the half-moon glow.

"I won't let my son run into the dark! No child of mine—"

My father's voice sliced through the yard. "But the boy is not afraid of the dark! He is afraid of us!"

And my mother let him go.

She watched Nachum run into the distance. She watched my father striding after him, following him down and around the block. Then she turned and came back inside.

I don't know how far my father walked that night. I don't remember how much time passed after I let go of the window-sill, but when the front door finally opened and my father stepped inside, Nachum followed quietly behind him.

Forty-Three

I slept most of the next morning. It was nearly noon when Aunt Zahava woke me. I ate a quick breakfast and then rode the bus to Jaffa Road, to the secondhand English bookstore. Then, at twenty to four, I returned to Aunt Itta's and walked up the hill and down again.

From afar, I saw Nachum waiting, peering closely at his digital watch. His legs shifted impatiently as he stood by the railing in front of the building. Then he looked up and saw me. He smiled, as if dazzled by my existence. He thrust his head forward, then the rest of his body followed, and he hurried up the slope to meet me.

I hugged him, touching him lightly. It was ten minutes past four. Nachum looked again at his watch.

"Ah, ah, ah—" he said. "So...so you came at four...and ten minutes." He waved his hand dismissively. "*Lo norah.* Never mind. Never mind. Ih-ih-ih-it's almost—it's almost still four...four o'clock."

Upstairs in the apartment, he offered me a drink.

"So, so, so, you want—you want *pih-petel*? Or jih—juice? Orange juice?"

I wanted *petel*. He filled my cup right up to the brim. I sipped from it quickly, so it wouldn't spill over. Then we went to the corner grocery. Aunt Itta needed eggs and milk.

In the small corner store, I watched him pick up the items, placing them carefully on the small conveyor belt. I watched him meticulously count out the change: four shekels for the milk, five for the eggs, and two and a half from his allowance for a bag of chips.

On the way home, I asked Nachum for some chips. He looked at me eagerly. "Ha, ha, ha—how many?" he asked.

I thought for a moment.

"One?" I suggested, unsure.

Nachum reached into the bag. He carefully took out one chip and gave it to me.

We walked half a block. Again, I asked for chips, but this time for a few.

"*Kih-kih-kih—kamah at rotzah?*" he asked. "Ha, ha, how many do you want?"

"Just a few," I answered, and thought I was being very clear.

Nachum looked at me, bewildered. He stared down at the bag as if it had turned into a mystery. His eyebrows furrowed. His mouth opened, then shut, then opened again.

I changed my mind.

"Two chips," I said. "Two."

Nachum reached into the bag, his brows unfurrowed, relief

on his face. He counted out two chips and carefully placed them in the palm of my hand.

"Thank you," I said.

He nodded vigorously, cheeks filled with potato chips. But at the steps of the building, with the bag nearly empty, I asked for three more.

I watched his hand searching in the bag, his fingers struggling to take out exactly three chips. This was tricky, because with his left hand he held the bag, and with his right hand he pulled out the chips—one, then two, then three. The third one cracked between his fingers.

So he started again. This time, he pulled some out randomly, but what came out was a handful of four. He frowned. He dropped the chips back in the bag.

His hand now rustled inside the bag in agitation. I could see the order of things becoming confused in his head. His hand and his entire mind were buried in the chaos of chips as he pulled out the first, the second, and the impossible third, which snapped again like a dry twig in his fingers.

My hand reached out slowly.

"Nachum," I said. "Nachum...I will try." Immediately, he pulled his fingers out of the bag and thrust it toward me as if handing over an impossible mission.

I pulled out a handful of chips, laying them out over my open palm. Then I counted out three with the other hand. The rest I dropped back in the bag, which I returned to my brother.

"Thank you," I said. "I have three chips."

My brother nodded once emphatically, reassuring himself that things were all right.

"You, you, you...you are welcome," he said.

Back upstairs, Aunt Itta gave us meringues. We stood by the window, sugar and egg whites melting in our mouths. The curtains rustled in the afternoon breeze as we looked out over the hills of Jerusalem.

Forty-Four

"Autism spectrum disorder," said the tall and important book, "is a complex neurodevelopmental disorder manifested across multiple contexts and characterized by severe deficit in social-emotional reciprocity, communication impairment, and repetitive patterns of idiosyncratic..." Blah, blah, blah.

I shut the book. It was impossible to understand, its pages filled with large words running busily across small, crowded lines.

I asked my cousin Batya how they had done it. How did Nachum change? She shrugged and smiled. She asked if I wanted more cake.

"Yes," I said. "More cake, please. But tell me, how did it happen?"

Batya bent over the stencil on the table, marking out a circle of dots for her kindergarten class.

"Prayers and miracles," she said. "And faith."

I shifted the couch pillow behind my back. Yes, yes, of course, prayers and miracles and lots of faith, but also something to do with the chart on the wall in Nachum's room, and the permanent scar on Ayalah's knee, engraved into her skin by my brother from the time when he did not have words. One did not just walk into a closed labyrinth where fearful children stood armed at the gates of their minds. Bad things happened to people who came looking.

I pushed the book away and sighed, bored, leaning against the armrest of the couch. I watched Batya fill in apples on her tree. There was still an hour until Nachum came home. Then we'd eat dinner and go to the Western Wall.

I asked Batya why Nachum still spoke funny. After all, if his mind had connected and his brain had somehow healed, why couldn't he talk the way I did? Why did he still stumble over sounds?

Batya put down the red marker she was holding, switching it for a green one. "Because it's hard for him to speak," she said.

"But why?" I asked.

"Because he's still autistic," she said.

"He's a cured autistic."

"Not exactly."

"Well, he's not crazy anymore."

"Okay."

"So?"

"He's still autistic."

"How?"

"His mind operates differently."

The marker brushed against the stencil in smooth, green strokes.

"I don't understand," I said. "How does his mind operate differently?"

Batya did not answer.

"And why does he still speak funny?"

She nodded her head, as if she'd heard, her eyes focused on the tree trunk.

"And why does he still pace when he gets very excited or nervous? Do you remember how he used to rock? Like a crazy boy? Why did he do that?" I curled my ponytail around my thumb, smoothing down the frizzy hair. "What does 'autistic' mean?"

The marker stopped. Batya looked up from her apple tree, its top now round and fully green. "Do you know why babies like being rocked?" she asked.

"Yes," I said. "Because they're babies."

"But why do they like it?"

"Because rocking is soothing."

"Yes. How?"

"The swaying. The back-and-forth moving."

Batya looked at me, as if waiting for more. "So?"

"What do you mean, 'So?'"

"What's the connection? Why do babies want to be rocked?"

I looked at her, exasperated. "Because they're *babies!*"

I flipped the pillow across the couch. Good Lord of the heavens and earth, what a question! Because that's how God made babies: for rocking.

But Batya said that rocking had nothing to do with size. It had to do with fear. It had to do with the balance between the senses that keep the world aligned.

"When a baby is born," she said, her voice filled with patience, "their vision is not focused. Everything is gray and blurry."

I rolled my eyes. I knew that.

"It's like suddenly all of space is filled with shades and shadows. There are strange, unpredictable sounds. Suddenly it's cold, then hot. There's this sharp light that stings the eye, and shapes loom in and out. Everything shifts and moves unexpectedly."

I knew that. Sort of.

Batya continued. "Rocking soothes a baby because it stops the jumble of movement and sounds. Now there is just one motion. Rocking is a simple, predictable rhythm that makes the body feel safe. It lets the mind shut out a world that the brain can't yet process. Rocking provides balance that the senses don't have."

She stopped to see if I understood. I nodded. I had definitely not known that. Nor did I know what it had to do with my brother. Because Nachum had rocked way past his baby years, way past the age when it was normal or remotely cute.

"But in babies," Batya went on, "vision slowly comes into focus. Over time, their minds adapt to the sounds around them. The ears, eyes, and fingers of a baby are like windows to the outside world opened just enough to take in the right amount of touch, light, and sound, so that the brain can process them. The child no longer needs the rocking, because the senses, now aligned, provide balance from inside. The baby feels secure. The world is a comfortable place that he can now explore."

Batya left the table and her tree drawing and sat down beside me on the couch. She picked up the flipped-over pillow and settled it on her lap.

"But not for your brother," she said. "For autistic children there is no balance. The senses never align. The mind is never safe—it can't ever settle down. It's not that they see too little; it's that they see too much. Their windows are open wide, much more than the average person—there is nothing to stop the heat and cold and rain from flooding inside. Touch, light, and sound rush in through their ears, eyes, and skin, but it's too much for their senses to process. Such a mind is a frenzied place, the brain battered and overwhelmed. Inside their heads there is always a terrible storm."

Batya stopped, allowing me to absorb her words.

"Do you realize what the world looks like to such a child?" she asked. "For your brother, the world was never a safe space to explore. It was a terrifying and dangerous place that he needed to fight off, endlessly."

I remembered Nachum's flailing hands, his frenzied eyes, and wondered for the first time what he'd seen when he looked at me. What kind of strange creature had I been? I remembered him holding up his hands, protecting his face as if he were being attacked by a swarm of bees, and I wondered: What had my hands felt like on his raw, bare skin? My poking finger, like the sharp point of a spear? What had my voice sounded like when I screamed?

A boy like that needed balance, and that's why he rocked. A mind like that needed silence, needed for the merciless earth to stop. It was like running through a corridor filled with looming, blurry faces, and frightening echoes that bounced off the walls. It was like opening door after door in long, endless hallways, and following a maze with no way out. The only thing to do was curl up in a corner, and rock.

Back. Forth.

Back. Forth.

Back. Forth.

Back. Until his brain had disconnected from his ears, until his eyes had stopped seeing the colors and light, until his body had ceased to absorb the world's signals, until he'd shut down every last switch of his mind. And inside it was dark and still.

Batya said it was called sensory deprivation. It said so in the tall book. She said it was the way autistic children survived. It was also the reason, she explained, that Nachum did not speak back then.

"When the brain shuts down, it does so completely. It cuts everything out—all the lights, all the sounds, both the music and the noise, the prodding hands and the gentle hugs. In such cacophony, the only relief is utter silence."

But still, I could not understand. Because I remembered the paintings my mother brought home a few months after Nachum left. She had hung them up proudly in our kitchen and entrance hall. There was a still life of wildflowers and apples, and canvases filled with rich shades of purple and red, petals unfurling toward the sun, specks of dancing sunlight mingling gracefully with the shadows—images no child his age should have been able to draw. Several of my brother's artworks had hung on the walls of the prime minister's official residence in Jerusalem, exhibited by ALUT, the Israeli Society for Autistic Children. When the exhibit was over, the painting came home to us in Brooklyn.

Nachum had always made impossible things: complicated Lego structures, delicate strokes of pastel color on drawing paper, like bright flashes of genius in a dark room. But I had never liked the pictures on the wall. They had stared down at me, a disturbing reminder of something gone terribly wrong. How could a boy who saw flowers and apples like that be so blind?

I asked Batya how it was possible. If all Nachum wanted to do was make himself unsee, how had he created the paintings on the wall? If he could turn himself deaf, how had he heard the bird chirping way up on the top of the tree in our back-yard, listening to it one morning for what had seemed like an hour, as if under a spell?

Batya told me to imagine a mind that worked like a mi-croscope. The same eyes that could be overwhelmed by an avalanche of signals could tune in to the smaller things that a normal mind could never perceive. A leaf, a flame, music, num-bers, particular patterns and details—his senses latched onto such things because he could see them with crystal clarity.

But that had not ever been a good thing.

"Nachum would sit with his eyes glued to the picture on

the Lego box," I told Batya. "Maybe he was seeing something clearly, but if I tried to touch him or if my father tried to help him with his Lego, he'd scream like he was being skinned alive."

Batya leaned forward, trying to make me see.

"Nachum's mind was in constant chaos, Menuchah. So when he finally found a thing that brought order to his senses, he held on to it like a drowning person to a branch. In a flame, in a running stream, in the pieces of his Lego—there was balance. His mind could process it, and it was like a tiny island of peace."

"But those things didn't even calm him down," I exclaimed. "They just tensed him up in a different way."

"Because like that," Batya said, snapping her fingers, "the balance could disappear. If he moved one wrong inch this way or that, the chaos would come tumbling in again."

I began to understand his paintings. In the drawings he had made, the way no child his age should have been able to, lay the excruciating details that Nachum perceived, like a map to his wide-open senses. Where I saw an apple on a tray, he saw varied shades of green, how the light flickered off the skin. Where I saw a fruit, he saw a pattern, a precise order of detail and shadow that became a single point of clarity in a world of utter chaos. It was this vision that had made him blind. Perhaps a drawing for Nachum had never been a work of art, but a distraction, an escape, a cry for help, a means of explaining the way he saw and why he could not speak. Strangely enough, Nachum stopped drawing as soon as he began to talk.

*   *   *

Later that evening, as my gentle cousin and I walked up and down hills and along narrow, twisting streets toward the open-air market on Machaneh Yehuda Street, Batya told me a story.

"In your brother's room," she said, "there hung a little red wig on the hook in the corner."

I shook my head, not understanding why she was telling me this. She continued.

"The first time your mother left Nachum in Israel, he would not let her go. We had to peel his fingers off her ankles so she could leave the house."

On the day my mother was to leave for the airport, my brother had held on to her, his fingers clasped around her wrists. He had thrown himself on the floor, his hands locked around her ankle in an ironlike grip as he screamed. Shaking and trembling, he had cried and begged, *"Ima! Ima! Ima! Ima!,"* because he did not want to be left behind.

My mother promised that she'd be back, but Nachum never heard her. She stroked his face and soothed his tears, swearing that she was not abandoning him, that in a few weeks she would return. But a boy like that could not understand; to him, words were meaningless sounds. He could not understand that in Israel there were resources that did not yet exist in New York; a family with older children and a place and their hearts to give him; and the Hebrew language through which he had once, if rarely, communicated.

Nachum had only his eyes with which he watched my

J u d y   B r o w n

mother leave, walk out the door, and drive away in the back of a cab on her way home to New York.

In the end, she had left him on the floor. Ayalah had held tightly to his right hand, my Aunt Itta to his left, while his kicking feet landed in Batya's bruising lap. This is how it was for a boy who had no words.

It was Dr. Cory Shulman who knew how to make him understand. The next time my mother arrived in Israel, Dr. Shulman explained how one makes a promise to a child with no words. She told my mother to make a pact with him. On the day she left, she and Nachum would exchange an item. My mother sat on his bed in his room, and my brother sat next to her. He gave her a knitted wallet he'd made, and she gave him an old red wig that she'd worn every day for as long as he could remember.

And my brother let her go. He watched calmly as she explained that she was leaving. He let her kiss him good-bye. He watched her walk out the door and down the stairs, and from the window he saw her sit in the back of the cab. Then he watched the cab drive up the hill and away, disappearing around the curve in the road. Afterward, he sat in his room and played with his Lego.

Because in my brother's mind, my mother was still there, in the piece of herself she'd left behind just for him. To him, the wig had never been something separate or apart; a person's hat or watch or the clothing they wore was part of their makeup the way their hands and legs were. The red wig worn by my mother was a piece of my mother, there, still in his room. Now she was not gone; it was only that most of her was somewhere else. This meant that she'd return, that she would always come back to him.

The red wig stayed in my brother's room for more than two years. It hung on the hook as a binding pact, a sacred promise, until he found a way to make one in words.

Forty-Five

At the Western Wall, I watched my brother pray. Through the narrow opening between the stones and the gate separating men from women, I could see my brother's profile, his forehead merging with the wall, his lips shaping the words of the prayer.

Around me, the whispers of a thousand voices rolled over the plaza like the murmur of the sea. In the crevices between stones the size of boulders, I could see the folded-up notes, pushed inside the gaps, each plea buried deep, awaiting the attention of the divine.

To my right, a young woman wept. Her face was buried in her prayer book, and her fist banged emphatically against the stones, as if she would not leave this place until God had changed His mind. Behind me, a group of marriage-age girls swayed fervently. When they finished, they brought their hands up to their lips and, reaching past me, touched the tear-stained slabs of rock. Then slowly they walked backward, still facing what remained of the ancient temple. One did not turn one's back on this wall.

I asked God to forgive me. I told Him that I knew now that He had never lied about the miracle. He'd kept His side of the bargain; it was I who had not. Because after those forty days, with my brother still as crazy as a bat, I'd been furious with God. I'd accused the heavens of taking my best prayers and giving nothing in return.

I asked God to forgive me. I'd been only eight, I whispered, and the miracles I knew of from the stories of the saints always happened within the hour—at most, after one month and seven days. So when my fast was over and nothing had changed, I turned away, and even as the miracle unfolded around me in the five years that followed, I had refused to look.

Some miracles take a long time. Some need more than forty days and nights; they take perhaps years of work and dedication. Some miracles unfold over time in stunning acts of transformation—a rock sculpted by wind and water, a seed turned into an oak, a mountain range pushed up, a canyon carved out. They're formed over years and centuries in stretched-out, slow-motion magic. Maybe you can't see it happening, but it is still a miracle.

I'd been an idiot, I told God from within the murmuring crowd. Because five years on, I finally realized that He had never said no. He had only said "Wait."

Forty-Six

There was no one particular incident that brought Nachum to words. It had been a gradual thing, occurring in the weeks and months of his second year at the school for autistic children. It was there that my brother began to speak.

Maybe it was the structure, the silent space, only possible without five demanding siblings around. Maybe it was the love and mind-bending devotion, the cocoon created within my aunt and uncle's home. Maybe it was the trained therapists who could see the storm in his head, or the experts who could translate the sounds of his silence and his screams. Or maybe it was prayers, pious deeds, and an abundance of faith.

Later on, a teacher would show me the cards they had used to break down the compendium of noise we call language and expression into small, comprehendible bits. She called it a manual for understanding sounds. She said that for my brother, words were not an instinct but a system to be taught and practiced, the way one learns how to swim or multiply numbers. So the flash card with the smiling face must be held up and defined clearly as "happy," the card with the frowning face as "sad," and a face with tears on its cheek as "cry."

Cry, cry, cry. Sad, sad, sad. Scared, excited, mad. These are the word-sounds for emotions, the way Nachum began decoding the shifting movements on other people's faces.

The teacher would stand with him in front of a mirror when he was confused, holding up the card with a confused face near his own, and repeat "confused" until Nachum had made the connection between the word-sound "confused"— the thing he felt inside himself—and the expression on his own face, or on other people's faces. When people grimaced a certain way, they were confused.

Until then, he could not know.

The flash cards were just one of several kinds of visual aids the school used to break down the chaos of the world into pieces that Nachum could process, and then build the pieces back up into patterns that he could understand. This was how the jumble of lights and noises was slowly untangled, separated into details he could fathom—every person, place, and thing a lesson of its own; every expression, emotion, and object put in meticulous order. The bewildering sensations that had once seemed to be trespassing on the territory of his life were now organized, defined, and labeled, word-sounds arranged in a mental toolbox. Until finally, there came a time when Nachum looked up and turned on the switches of his mind.

* * *

"You can't reorder the senses of an autistic person," Batya said. "But you can teach him to define what his ears and eyes bring into his head. You can teach him to better understand the messages, the difference between loud sounds that are threats and ones that are just running bathwater, between a looming object that means danger and a hand reaching out to help. You can make the earth a safer place for him to explore, and slowly his brain can settle and begin to absorb."

Nachum began to hear words, and perhaps it was then that he learned to fend off the outside without completely shutting it out. My brother learned fast, first tens, then hundreds, then thousands of words in less than a year. It was as if once his mind had begun to grasp the connection between sounds and meanings, he wanted to absorb them all.

Words were like a secret he'd unearthed, revealing the instructions for living on this mysterious planet. Words were a code that, when finally deciphered, directed him in the ways and manners of a foreign planet. Words made every experience less frightening, more predictable, and the ceaseless background noise finally quieted down.

"But why does he still talk funny?" I asked.

"Well," retorted Batya, "have you tried learning French?"

"No," I said. "But if I would, I'd talk like the French."

"You barely talk Hebrew like the Hebrew."

"I most certainly do."

"No, dear cousin, you don't."

"I definitely talk Hebrew like the Hebrew."

Batya shrugged, her eyes teasing.

"My Hebrew isn't funny," I said, annoyed.

"It isn't *very* funny," she agreed.

"It isn't funny at all."

"It's a *little* funny. With a bit of New York wrapped inside Israel."

"I speak a perfect Hebrew Hebrew."

"You do?"

"Mostly, I do."

Batya's eyebrow curved up. She laughed.

"Okay," I said. "Maybe I have a tiny accent."

"Yes, maybe."

I sniffed.

"Anyway, what does this have to do with Nachum's Hebrew?" I demanded, arms folded over my chest. "He's been living here for years, and he still speaks funny."

Batya laughed out loud.

"It's not his English or his Hebrew. It's language—it's words."

"Huh?"

"It's words," she repeated. "Words are foreign to your brother. Communication itself is like a second language. The work you'd need to put in to learn French, he needed to put in to learn human."

I shook my head, but Batya was not done yet.

"Nachum did not become magically unautistic. He is not 'cured.' He never will be. He became fluent in the human language by rote memorization and practice, but it's still a second language. So he'll always have an accent."

I stood up and walked to the windows overlooking the hills. Outside, little cabs with yellow lights drove by, their fenders disappearing around the bends of the twisting roads. On the sidewalk, boys in *kippas* ran screaming, chasing after balls that bounced down the slope. Near the steps, ponytailed girls in long skirts and button-down shirts giggled and jumped, chanting the words of an old Hebrew rhyme. I watched a white van pull up to the entrance of our building. The doors folded inward like an accordion and my brother Nachum came out.

I sighed. I knew that Batya was right—about Nachum, not about my accent. It wasn't as if I hadn't known any of this at all. I'd heard these things before, vaguely. My mother had said them at some point, but I had never listened. I'd never read *My Special Brother,* the book she had bought me, or watched the movie *Rain Man,* about an autistic brother. I'd never read Nachum's painstaking first letter home to us, and I hadn't remembered the name of the school he had attended.

It was as though I had been living on a tiny island with only two mountains and a chasm in between. On one side stood my determined mother, and on the other everyone else. I stood with everyone else. The people on my side of the chasm saw what my brother had as a frightful disease. They feared it, and I absorbed the fear. They loathed it, and so did I. They called it a curse because they did not have the words to explain it, and where there are no words, there is always fear.

Forty-Seven

Nachum and I met a girl on the way to Aunt Itta's house. It was a week after I'd arrived in Israel, and my brother had picked me up from Aunt Zahava's apartment after school. I saw the tall, thin girl with an easy smile from afar, as we walked past Tnuva's dairy factory.

"Nachum," she said, surprised. "How are you? Is this your sister?"

Nachum's eyes flashed. He stammered with excitement.

"I, I, I...I am fine. Vih-very much. Thank God...And, and, and, and...thi-this, this, *this* is my sister, Meh-nuchah. She, she...*she* is my sister." At the word "sister," a smile spread wide across his dimpled face.

"Ahh," said the girl, "so this is your sister." She turned to me and gave me a welcoming hug. She said it was so nice to meet me. Nachum had been telling her for weeks that soon, soon I'd come.

I nodded politely. "Ahh, *ken, nechmad*. How nice. I was really excited to come."

*　　*　　*

"Who *is* that girl?" I asked as we walked away.

"Thi-that, thi-that is Matty. She takes me to the park. Every week...to play."

In the fifteen minutes that it took to walk down the hill to his street, my brother introduced me to four different strangers.

"Thi-this, this, this...*this* is my sister, Meh-nuchah...She, she, she is my sister. My sister."

I should have been embarrassed. After all, it wasn't as though Nachum was normal. But strangely, I didn't care. Instead, I found myself observing him curiously, wanting to know every detail of his world. Suddenly, I didn't think in terms of the levels of crazy. My brother had emerged unexpectedly from a distant legend. Overnight, he had stopped being a character and become my brother. I had crossed the sea that separated his life from mine, and now I found that his story was mine too. I was his sister, to the man selling papers on the corner, to the girl who took him to the park, to myself.

I watched him in awe.

"And who was that?" I asked Nachum of the third person we had stopped to talk to who now knew that I was his sister Meh-nuchah.

"He, he, he—he is a man who is a seller of fih-lowers. Seller of fih-lowers. Uncle Zev buys fih-lowers there, fih-lowers every Shabbat."

"And that man who is waving?"

"He…he, he. Is a man. Just. A man. I do, do not know. He is fih-riendly…for no good reason at all."

We crossed the road. Instinctively, I took his hand. Nachum studied our linked hands.

"You, you, you…you are holding my hand."

"I am." I explained, "I am being careful about the cars. Because you are my brother."

"Yih-yes. Yih-yes, yes," he quickly agreed. "I am—I am your brother. When we cross, you will put your hand in mine." The dimpled smile appeared as though he agreed that indeed, this was a good idea.

I thought about what I'd done. I realized that my brother crossed the streets of Jerusalem by himself every day, all the time. He really did not need me to hold his hand. And maybe this occurred to him too. Because suddenly he chuckled, as though it was funny, as though he remembered something.

"Be, be, because I am your brother…your cih-razy brother."

I cringed. "What? Wha-what? No. You are not."

He giggled gleefully, as if teasing me. "Yes, yes, yes, yes. I…I…I am your brother. Your cih-razy, *crazy* brother."

He laughed out loud. He shook my hand hard, as if that would explain his words. I looked at him, taken aback. Then I giggled, just a little. It was hard not to, seeing his expression. He was so utterly pleased with what he had said.

"I am *cih-razy,* your cu-cuckoo, tru-la-lu-lah—bih-rother."

I laughed now along with him, because it was funny, what I had called him back at home—and he had known.

"We are all a little crazy," I said.

303

He chuckled, liking this, striding yards ahead of me before realizing he had dropped my hand and I was no longer next to him. Then he turned around and marched back up to me.

"We all are, we all are," he repeated. "Cih-razy. Also Ayalah, and also Aunt Itta, and also Batya. But only I...I...I—only I am your cih-razy brother. Your cih-razy brother."

I agreed. "Only you are my crazy brother. My favorite, crazy one."

He guffawed, his head lurching forward as he strode down the hill, far ahead of me.

Forty-Eight

My grandmother Savtah Miriam fumbled with the watch on her swollen wrist. She sat down heavily in the armchair by her bed.

"She was standing on the threshold of her apartment," she told me. "'Enough with the tears,' she had said. 'The rebbe has given his blessing.'"

Savtah Miriam's hands quivered as she recalled standing outside her mother-in-law Bubba Miril's home on Sanhedrin Street, some twenty years before.

"Come inside," Bubba Miril had said. "Sit down, Miriam. Let's talk."

But my grandmother shook her head, no. "Not until you promise that the rebbe will take back his blessing."

Savtah Miriam reached out for the clear glass teacup in my hand. She was nearly seventy years old and struggling with the onset of Parkinson's. She leaned forward stiffly. I bent closer, waiting for the spasms to stop long enough for her fingers to grasp the cup. Slowly, she lifted the tea to her mouth. Her lips twitched and trembled but her dark, still-lovely eyes gazed at me calmly.

"Your mother was a beauty," she said, watching the sugar settle in the cup. "All my daughters were."

I sat on my grandmother's bed while she sipped the warm liquid, a rivulet of tea seeping from the corner of her mouth. Even with the windows wide open, the apartment smelled like a hospital room. Pharmacy bottles and pill containers were scattered everywhere among scented lotions and brand-name perfumes. Behind the jar of Vaseline lay a string of South Sea pearls. It dangled off the edge of the bedside table like an old, forgotten toy.

The phone rang shrilly on Savtah Miriam's lap. Gripping the receiver, she poked at the talk button with her jumping pointer finger. Then, as if urging her limb to lift itself, she yanked her arm upward, tilted her head, and leaned her ear into the phone.

It was Dr. Shachor, her gerontologist, the one she'd called four times since the morning. This would be a long conversation. I left my grandmother on the phone and went off to the adjacent room, the former master bedroom, where she no longer slept. I searched through the leftovers of her past. It was my third visit to her home since I'd come to Israel, but I was still nowhere near done exploring.

Inside closets guarded by iron keyholes and old skeleton keys, glamorous dresses hung in dry-cleaning wrappers, some still with receipts that had been stapled on a decade before. From the musty drawers of a dresser last polished before I was born, I pulled out antique watches with leather bands, gold brooches that I tried pinning on my cotton shirt, and silky scarves that I twirled around my still-chubby neck. All around me were my grandmother's things, the clothes and shoes of her younger years: four-inch heels tottering in the corner, a mound of skirts thrown over a chair, cashmere cardigans folded neatly in hopeful piles, waiting to be worn again. There were belts and shawls sorted and wrapped in plastic bags, perhaps waiting to be given to the poor, while four musty wigs on Styrofoam heads observed it all from their pedestals on the windowsill.

In this room, years before, my grandfather and grandmother had slept, and their master bedroom furniture was untouched among the piles of folded-up memories. In the corner by the window, packed carefully into boxes, lay porcelain cups and hand-painted dishes, brought from America as gifts by my grandfather at least two decades before.

I could hear my grandmother bid the doctor good day and end the call. Then the shrill ringtone pierced the air again. It was one of my aunts, or maybe a friend of Savtah Miriam's. I stuffed the silk scarves back in a drawer and closed the door behind me, moving into the living room.

During my second visit to my grandmother's apartment, I had found albums and containers filled with photos in the buffet cabinet against the wall, beneath the elegant glass cups and silverware. I had opened the albums and begun to look, but then Batya had come to pick me up—it had been almost four—so I'd left, reluctantly.

Sitting on the floor now, I pulled out three albums—one with a red cover, one beige, and one an ugly green—from the shelf. I waited quietly by the threshold. Then, as my grandmother continued to complain on the phone about her aches and pains, I quickly crossed her open doorway and stepped into the kitchen. I was afraid that if she saw me with the albums, she'd tell me to put them back.

In the cabinet near the fridge were shopping bags that my grandmother always kept bursting with cookies and sweets. I broke off two rows of a chocolate bar and grabbed a handful of licorice and two hazelnut cream wafers. Then I sat on the wooden chair at the tiny kitchen table, teeth drowning in sugar, and opened the first of the three wedding albums.

Suddenly I noticed the silence. From my grandmother's room came the sounds of birds chirping on the window ledge and slippered feet scuffing the floor in boredom. My grandmother had hung up the phone.

"Menuchah!" she called from across the hall. "Bring the albums here."

I jumped up and walked to her room, the albums cradled in my arms like a cache of ill-gotten goods.

"Bring them here," Savtah Miriam said eagerly, her hand fluttering in the air. "Sit down next to me. I haven't seen these in years."

So I laid out the albums on her bed: red, beige, and ugly green. She pointed to the green.

"That's your mother's," she said.

I opened the album on her lap. She touched it gently with a trembling hand. The muscles in her neck balked and strained as if in deliberate resistance. Her face flinched, the tendons in her cheeks shuddering, as she forced herself forward. Finally, her body eased, as if agreeing only reluctantly to let my grandmother back into her past.

Savtah Miriam smiled when she saw herself, porcelain skin and designer clothes, once queen of the neighborhood. She turned the page, her eyes wide open as if it was pitch-dark. Aunt Tziporah looked up at us from a photo, the accordion folds of her pink silk dress covering her expectant stomach. In another photo stood a group of friends wearing their hair piled high like beehives, old-fashioned pumps, and dresses with loud, colorful patterns. And there was my great-aunt Frieda, her arm around my patient mother's waist, her other hand clutching a shimmering rhinestone purse. Nearby, a circle of women danced as my grandmother, in her rippling silver and mint-green gown, looked on.

I pointed to a photo of all three sisters: Chana, Zahava, and my mother.

"Who made Chana's *shidduch*?" I asked.

My grandmother searched the picture, her voice foundering but certain. "God in Heaven," she said. "Who else?"

She paused and then added, "Also Yankiv, the shadchan, and Wiessmandel, the rebbe's assistant, who knew the boy."

"Who made Zahava's *shidduch*?" I asked.

Savtah Miriam shook her head, as though I was asking all the wrong questions. "God in Heaven," she repeated. "Who else?"

"And who made my mother's *shidduch*?" I asked, my finger resting on my mother's tiara in the photo.

"Your mother's *shidduch*?"

"My mother's *shidduch*."

Savtah Miriam's head swayed. "Your mother," she said. "Your aunt. Also your father."

My finger stayed on my mother's tiara. Savtah Miriam looked down, waiting for it to move. When it did not, she looked up at me, her eyes lingering.

"God in Heaven, of course," she said, as though her earlier words had been a careless mistake. "Don't bite your lips like that. It makes you less pretty."

We looked through the rest of the album, which contained most of the same photos we had back home. I pointed to one of my favorites, of my grandfather between my mother and father, all their faces aglow.

"They look happy," I said.

Savtah Miriam leaned closer. "They are happy," she said. "They were very close."

"Who?" I asked.

She waved a shaky finger over the picture. "They. It was the happiest day of Sabah's life when he married off your mother, his youngest daughter." My mother looked out from beneath the protective plastic, her hand touching her chin, on her finger the diamond ring. I chuckled as I looked at the picture, and Savtah Miriam wanted to know why, but I said that it was nothing—just a joke I'd remembered. Because it was hard to explain to my grandmother the things I'd been told as a child.

"Your father bought the most expensive jewelry," Savtah was saying, smiling at the memories. "Nobody had jewelry like Esther. You know that he worked for a year in New York, sending her gifts back here in Israel?"

Peering at another photo of my parents, she cleared her throat and then said, as if in approval, "Your father was a handsome man."

I chuckled again, agreeing. I had always known that. Even as a child, I had understood that if among the characters in fairy tales were Chassidim, and if among those Chassidim two were allowed to fall in love, then the princess bride and soldier groom chosen for the picture on the cover would look like my beautiful mother and my father, tall and slender, with high cheekbones and merry eyes, always laughing as if at a secret joke.

Savtah Miriam gazed at the album as if she'd forgotten I was there, as if she were still standing under the canopy beside my mother, with her husband and my father to their left, everyone's eyes closed in prayer.

"Oh, how he loved him," she said. "He always said that he was like a son. He was his favorite one..."

Then she came back out of the picture, and saw me again. She took a piece of licorice from my hand and chewed it slowly, savoring the sweetness, her eyes moving from me to the album and back, as if deciding whether to worry about what I had heard her say. Then she shrugged, or maybe it was the Parkinson's tossing her shoulder about.

"Such things you don't say out loud," she said, and repeated it once more. "You don't say out loud."

We turned the page. There was the Holy Rebbe and, to his right, his brother, the one who'd be rebbe after him. There was my other great-great-uncle and, at his side, my grandfather, shaking a well-wisher's hand. In between them sat my father, with his trimmed beard and tall, fur hat, a soldier in a Chassid's land.

"So the rebbe gave a blessing?" I asked.

Savtah Miriam did not answer.

"So did the rebbe give a blessing?" I asked.

She paused, as if absorbing my question. Then she answered, "Of course he gave a blessing."

"But why," I asked, "if my father wasn't yet a Chassid?"

"Of course he was a Chassid," she said, her eyes squinting and then widening so that I could not tell her meaning.

"Always?" I asked.

"Always," she answered. "In the soul. For marriage, he added only the hat."

I looked down at the picture, at the first night my father, now a married man, had worn the fur *shtreimel,* and I heard my grandmother laugh, the tremors in her voice making it ripple and echo.

"What doesn't one do for love?"

I laughed along with her, but it wasn't because of the love. I laughed at the fear I'd been carrying around since third grade, since the day Blimi had said that awful thing about love.

It had been hard not to believe that over my family there hovered a dark curse. It had been just as hard to accept, though, that between my parents, who liked each other in all the right ways, there was some kind of wrong love. So after Nachum left home, I had stopped thinking about it entirely. Afraid to ask my parents or aunts if it was true, I never discussed it again. As I grew, I mostly forgot, a large enough part of my mind assuming that it was nonsense. The other part of my mind, smaller and much farther back, I ignored. Because there, gathering dust in the corner, the curse still loomed. What if it was real?

It was as though Savtah Miriam assumed that I already knew the first half of the story. Her voice quavered, dipping and sloping, words stopping just short of her tongue as she dropped memories of that time like a trail of crumbs for me to follow.

"Your great-grandmother, Bubba Miril, met your father first. She trusted your mother, and after a while, she agreed to speak with him. Your mother was no longer a girl of eighteen. She was already twenty-three.

"Bubba Miril agreed to speak with him, and when that happened, I knew it was over. Your great-grandmother was a smart, smart woman. Did you know that? The rebbe was her brother and he trusted her the way his Chassidim trusted him. They talked every single day. She was the real rebbe in the family.

"She told the uncles to meet your father. She said it was good, so of course they approved. The rebbe gave his final blessing. For your grandfather it was enough—his mother's approval. But not for me.

"She was a wise woman. Did you know that? Don't bite your lips like that. It makes you less pretty."

So in the end, it was Bubba Miril who made it happen. She had stood at the threshold of her apartment on Sanhedrin Street.

"Enough with the tears," she said to her daughter-in-law. "Your uncle, the rebbe, has given his blessing. Come inside. Sit down, Miriam. Let's talk."

But Miriam shook her head, no. "Not until you promise that the rebbe will take back his blessing."

"So what happened then, Savtah? What happened then?"

"Your great-grandmother was a very wise woman."

"But what happened then?"

"She got angry."

"Really? Bubba Miril?"

"She got very angry."

"Did she scream?"

"Bubba Miril never screamed. She did not speak much. She only said what there was to say."

"And what did she say?"

"She said what she said. She spoke in Yiddish. You know Yiddish? Of course you know Yiddish. *'Bashert iz nish vus macht dich frietig. Es iz nisht vus macht dehm sh'chainim frietig. Es iz nur vus macht deh himmel frietig.'* At mevinah, Menuchah? You understand?"

I understood. The words meant, "*Bashert* is not what pleases you. It is not what pleases the neighbors. It is only what pleases Heaven."

The other thing Bubba Miril said, also in Yiddish, was, "It is not for you to cry, Miriam. Sometimes the Almighty makes things happen, because the matchmakers won't. The rebbe will officiate at the wedding."

"So did you stop crying, Savtah?"

"Over time."

"How much time?"

"Enough time. There was a full year until the wedding. In between, your father sent your mother the most beautiful jewelry. Nobody in the entire city of Jerusalem got the gifts your mother did."

"You liked the jewelry?"

"Who could not like such jewelry?"

"Did you also like my father?"

"Your father was a very hardworking man. Everyone liked him."

"And were you happy about the wedding?"

"I was."

"As happy as you'd been about Zahava's wedding?"

"Just as much."

"Were you, really?"

"Of course I was! Do you have any idea how much that silver gown cost?"

Around me I saw the spirits smiling.

Forty-Nine

In the summer of 1975, the youngest of the Strauss sisters was married in Jerusalem. Hundreds arrived at the wedding, some to eat, some to stare, some because they were invited.

The rebbe, who had been staying in the northern city of Haifa for the summer, traveled back to Jerusalem for the chuppah. Flanked by his attendants and an entourage of Chassidim, he strode into the hushed courtyard outside the wedding hall. On his head he wore a shtreimel, *the fur hat worn on the Shabbos and for family celebrations.*

Beneath the canopy my father and grandfather stood, swaying fervently, their lips moving, their eyes closed in prayer. The chazzan leading the ceremony looked up at the skies, his voice rising and wailing as he sang the sacred song of marriage. The crowd turned toward the veiled bride as she walked down the aisle, accompanied by Savtah Liba on her left and Savtah Miriam on her right. In the seats lining the right side of the courtyard, my mother's and father's sisters gathered, wiping away tears of joy and murmuring prayers.

*The rebbe stood on the platform in front of the assembled
guests. In his right hand, he held a silver cup brimming with
wine. His voice rose as he intoned the blessing of betrothal, announcing to the heavens and to those on earth that the bride and
groom were now man and wife:*

בָּרוּךְ אַתָּה יְ-יָ אֱלֹהֵ-ינוּ מֶלֶךְ הָעוֹלָם, אֲשֶׁר קִדְּשָׁנוּ בְּמִצְוֹתָיו וְצִוָּנוּ עַל הָעֲרָיוֹת
וְהִתִּיר לָנוּ אֶת הַנְּשׂוּאוֹת לָנוּ עַל יְדֵי חֻפָּה וְקִדּוּשִׁין. בָּרוּךְ אַתָּה יְ-יָ, מְקַדֵּשׁ עַמּוֹ
יִשְׂרָאֵל עַל יְדֵי חֻפָּה וְקִדּוּשִׁין!

Blessed are you, Lord our G-d, king of the universe, who
has sanctified us with His commandments . . . Blessed are
you, Lord, who sanctifies His people Israel through
chuppah and kiddushin!

*Beneath the canopy, the groom placed a ring on the bride's
finger.*

הֲרֵי אַתְּ מְקֻדֶּשֶׁת לִי...

With this ring, you are consecrated to me . . .

*A glass cup was shattered underfoot. The crowd rose, the mu-
sic burst forth. Now the daughter of leaders and rabbis and the
son of a milkman and his widow were bound forever as one.*

*Savtah Miriam lifted the veil off her youngest daughter's face,
folding it back over her covered red hair. The newlyweds stepped
off the platform, and together they walked through the courtyard, besieged by happy strangers and friends shouting "Mazel
tov! Mazel tov!" from every side. It was then, when they reached
the hallway that led away from the crowd and to the room of
seclusion—where they'd eat their first meal as a couple, signi-
fying their new status as husband and wife—that my mother
turned around.*

She found her father, standing among the well-wishers a short distance away. He looked up and smiled, as his eyes reached out to her over the noise and the music. His face was filled with love and joy.

The photographer raised his camera. He zoomed in and pressed the button lightly. The shutter snapped and clicked, exposing the film. The moment stopped, their smiles froze, captured forever.

Fifty

One year later
October 16, 1994

It is Succoth, the last of the High Holidays. On my grandmother's roof porch in Jerusalem, it is night. The moon casts
a faraway glow over the tiled courtyard, which is festooned
with lights.

There are linen-covered tables set out on the porch, laid
with silverware and dishes enough for several dozen men. Inside, in the dining room, the women and girls—a small gathering of family, teachers, and my mother's closest friends—
will eat.

Because tonight is Nachum's bar mitzvah, the night he
turns thirteen. In the morning, he'll put on tefillin and join
the men in their prayers at shul. Next Shabbos, he'll walk to
the synagogue beside my Uncle Zev, wearing a hat like my fa-

ther's on his head. From this moment on, my brother is no longer a mere child. Tonight, he becomes a man.

A week before the Succoth holiday, my family—my parents, Aunt Tziporah, and we five siblings—flew to Israel from New York. Nearly every day, I watched Uncle Zev and my brother, studying the laws and rituals of tefillin, the black leather cubes containing scriptural passages that men attach to the arm and head and wear during morning prayers. On the day of the bar mitzvah, my cousins, sisters, Nachum, and I rode the bus to the Western Wall to pray.

Along the Western Wall, among the kiosks selling souvenirs and handmade crafts, I had planned to buy a gift for my brother from Kathy. Before I left New York, she had given me ten dollars to buy "something holy" for Nachum on his special thirteenth birthday. "Sure," I had said. "I'd be happy to do so." And I'd wondered what my brother would say.

But my brother did not remember Kathy. When I asked him a few days after we arrived what he wanted as a gift from Kathy, the neighbor upstairs, he said, "Who? Who?"

"Kathy," I said. "The goy who lives upstairs."

Nachum looked at me intently, as if trying to conjure up a person in his mind.

"Kathy," I reminded him again. "You know, in the attic apartment. She's big—like *this* tall—with red curly hair..."

Nothing.

"She's the *goy!*" I repeated impatiently. "Who lives upstairs, in that attic apartment, with Mark—her *goy husband.*"

But the more I pressed him, the more agitated he became, until, eyes blinking anxiously, feet shifting back and forth, he said, "*Loh, loh.* I do not, I do not, I do not remember. I do not wih-want to talk. Anymore."

And I stopped, because it made me scared to see him this way, a bit of how he used to be.

It took my brother all afternoon to calm down. And it took me a few days to comprehend what I'd done. I'd forced his mind back with my questions to a dark and distant place, to a time before he had words—and with them, the capacity to form coherent memories. In the fragmented existence of his younger years, people had been indistinct beings. Neighbors, cousins, family friends had slipped right past him, deflected off his overwhelmed mind as just other fragments in the chaos. To him, they hadn't been real at all.

So in the kiosk near the Western Wall, I had bought, in the end, a small gift for myself, hoping that Kathy's Jesus would forgive me even if my own God wouldn't. Then I joined my cousins praying at the wall, before we returned home to prepare for the celebration.

My cousins, sisters, and I put on our holiday dresses and elegant shoes. We sat patiently in leather chairs at the local hair salon. We ate a late lunch, and said the mincha afternoon prayers. Then we went to my grandmother Miriam's apartment, up on the third floor, and waited for the others to come.

Less than an hour later, I watched my brother walk ever so cautiously up the steps to my grandmother's apartment, as if the new hat, set perfectly on his head for the first time, would topple right off if he was any less careful. My mother, uncle, and aunt followed close behind him, laughing, calling out to us, their faces beaming, their hands gesturing excitedly at "this prince, this boy—look at him. Just look at him. So tall, so handsome..."

My brother, dressed in the immaculate long, dark silk *kapotah* coat worn by every Chassidic boy after his bar mitzvah, smiled shyly as he nervously fingered the braided belt tied around his waist. He showed us the dark velvet bag, cradled in the crook of his arm, that held his tefillin, and inside them the four scrolls inscribed with verses from the Torah.

At five thirty sharp, the caterer arrived. Savtah Miriam, in her sky-blue suit and flat, orthopedic slippers, her wig perfectly coiffed, her makeup already applied, shuffled slowly inside and out, her voice rising and wavering as she purposefully ordered the help around. At six fifteen, it was done: the glasses were standing like little soldiers, every plate, chair, and piece of silverware in order. On the stove in the kitchen sat large pans covered with foil to keep the food warm. The smell of *burekas,* chicken, and schnitzel wafted out into the hallway.

Uselessly, my sisters and I wandered about, trying not to

wrinkle our dresses. My cousins sat outside in the breeze, chatting with Savtah Miriam about this and that, as my mother rushed in and out of rooms, yelling at anyone there to be yelled at about the flowers that had come an hour late, the third cousins whom she should have invited, and my father, who—in the name of heaven—would not stop eating the schnitzels meant for the evening meal!

My father said he had had only three schnitzels. My mother did not care. As she grabbed the phone to call the photographer and demand to know the reason he was not there yet, I snuck a fourth schnitzel for my father. Back in the hallway, my mother brushed from Nachum's shiny coat the dust particles that could be seen only if you yourself were a dust particle.

At seven, the photographer, his equipment set up and ready on the porch, ordered us to stand and look happy—"No, happier. What is this, a funeral? Everyone laugh! Now!"—but my mother, worried about the time and the guests coming any minute, managed only a tense smile. My sister Rivky, nervous because my mother was, attempted a more cheerful look to cover her grimace. And my father, sweating in the impossible heat and filled to the brim with schnitzel, looked at the forced smile stretched across my anxious face and burst out laughing.

The photographer put up a triumphant hand.

"Like that! Like that! Now *that* is a smile!" And the shutter snapped and flashed at the six laughing brothers and sisters posing together by the gate outside, our backs to the setting sun. Savtah Miriam, sitting in the middle, smiled widely, her quivering lips for the moment calm and still.

Not one minute later, the guests began to arrive: uncles, cousins, family friends, several teachers, and Dr. Cory Shulman. My mother welcomed the women, directing them to the right side of the hall; my father welcomed the men to the left.

At 8 p.m., the elderly rebbe—the youngest of the rabbinical brothers, who had taken over after their deaths—arrived, and a respectful silence spread quickly through the apartment and across the roof. As he walked through the entrance hall, he turned to my grandmother, standing nearby, and murmured, "Mazel tov." He turned to my mother, nodded, and wished her *nachas*. Then, led by my uncle, he went onto the porch and sat at the small head table, where my brother and father stood, waiting.

My sisters and I rushed out from the dining room to watch. Tittering excitedly, we squeezed onto the narrow threshold among my mother, cousins, and aunts, and peered out onto the porch, where the men sat.

In the years that followed, and during the ups and downs that followed with them, I would remember every moment of this night. In the two decades that came after the bar mitzvah, as I watched my brother navigate the painful course from autistic child to autistic adult, I'd pull out this memory often—a scene of crowded tables and festive lights, of smiling cousins and laughing aunts, of my brother, sitting calmly, his back erect, with my father, the rebbe, and Uncle Zev. I'd remember Nachum's eyes moving over the crowd, carefully observing his surroundings. I'd remember how he shook each well-wisher's hand, nodding, listening, responding to the movements of faces and heads. And I'd remember the shadows on the stone ledge behind his table, shifting under the light of the lamps and the moon. My father's dark form bending slowly toward my brother, my brother's profile turning up to my father, and the moment their foreheads touched. And on the wall the shadows merged, becoming one.

What had been achieved that night was not perfection, but a miraculous new normal. Perhaps it was a normal still full of complexity; perhaps there would always be challenges and uncertainty. But on that night, my brother had done all that had been declared impossible: he had listened, he had heard, he had connected; he had become a man. Every hurdle that came afterward became a possible thing to overcome.

Aunt Itta stood between Ayalah and my mother, the glasses still crooked on the bridge of her nose. Their eyes followed my brother's every move, as if hypnotized. Batya, leaning against me, held my hand, squeezing it hard. I looked at her flushed face and smiled. She wore a simple dress and a small silver pendant around her neck. In front of her, Ayalah wore a dark suit and small pearl earrings.

I looked carefully at my two cousins, aunt, and uncle, who were basking in a quiet glow. There was nothing that set them apart, this family from the fourth floor on Rabbi Holy Man Street. There was nothing that said that, though they lived in a small, unair-conditioned apartment, they had one day taken an autistic boy into their home, entered his world, and refused to leave without him.

I looked up at the moon. The stars winked at me from their faraway places, scattered in the darkness like pairs of watchful eyes. I could hear voices murmuring in the background, the men singing *niggunim* of old.

I wondered if God could see us now, if He was looking down from on high at His carefully placed soul. Perhaps beside Him was the angel who had tapped too hard on Nachum's lip. Maybe around them were the other higher souls, all returned from their long journeys on earth among specially chosen families.

I wondered if my ancestors were watching, if Sabah Menachem Baruch could see what had become of the boy carrying his name. I imagined him smiling, his face filled with pride and joy. Perhaps it had been my grandfather who had gathered my ancestors, who had called for them to come, even as my mother stood over their graves, crying, pleading for help from above. Had Sabah Mechel, Bubba Miril, the Knesset minister, and the Holy Rebbes marched and marched toward the Almighty, breaking down the gates of Heaven? Perhaps they'd declared, "Enough! Enough with the suffering! Let the boy speak! Let him pray! Release this child's soul!"

Perhaps. It is really impossible to know. But whatever the reasons were, and whichever tales were true, one thing was certain: in a place where there unfolds such a miracle, there could never have been a curse.

Standing on my grandmother's roof, where she'd screamed

some twenty years before, her shame echoing over the neighbors' yards, I knew that it had really happened. That there, up above the clouds by the royal throne, God and his angels had gathered. There, forty days before my father and mother were born, a heavenly voice had called out, declaring,

"Esther Strauss, daughter of Menachem Baruch, granddaughter of Bubba Miril, descendant of rabbis and holy men, will fall in love with Shloimy, son of Mechel the milkman and his destitute, long-suffering wife, Faigah. Because such are the mysteries of Heaven, and this is what is meant to be."

And so it was.

It's true. It says so in the Talmud. Only God knows the secrets of love.

Epilogue

My brother has no memories from the time he could not speak. I know because I've asked him many times. The last time I did so was in early 2014, a few months before this manuscript's completion. I asked my brother if he remembered the summer he returned to Israel, five years before his bar mitzvah.

His reply was terse: "I do not remember that far past in time. I remember after my bar mitzvah, something like maybe ten years before your wedding."

It was the first time I'd asked Nachum about a memory in over two years. I knew I shouldn't have, that he hated it when I forced him back to that place. Several times as a teenager I had prodded him with my questions, poking and pushing him back into the past.

"*Atah zocher*? Do you remember when I broke the plate and blamed you? Do you remember the shul we went to on Fifty-First? Do you remember Kiki, the therapist with the bright red hair?"

Nachum did not remember. His mind had let go of the memories that had no words to explain them. He could see the first ten years of his life in pieces, the chain on the bike, the shreds of balloon in the branches of a tree, chairs piled up, higgledy-piggledy, in the shul backyard. For such a boy, an attempt to access memories was like a painful extraction.

Once, in Israel, I pushed too hard.

"*Atah zocher?*" I asked him as we walked downhill toward home. "Do you remember in the country, the picnic we had near the lake, with the geese?" But it was my fifth question, and Nachum reared back like an untamed colt.

"*Loh, loh, loh.* No, no, no. I, I, I dih-do not remember nih-nothing, nih-nothing, nih-nothing!"

I watched my brother march away from the places he could not understand and the things he could not remember: objects, voices, parts of faces, pieces floating in a vacuum.

When I was sixteen years old, I met such a boy again.

Chaim was four, an ultraorthodox child who lived a few blocks from our house in Brooklyn. Once a week on the Sabbath, my friend and I would take him out for a walk or to play for a couple of hours. We did this as part of a high school volunteer program. Chaim was autistic, the fourth of six children, and his mother really needed the break.

Chaim did not speak. Often, when we walked up the street, he'd hum a quiet tune to himself, as if this substituted for the words he did not have. But sometimes Chaim did not sing.

Instead, he'd stop walking and stand rigid and still, as if waiting for us to understand what he wanted. When we didn't, he'd sit down, little feet folded under him on the cold asphalt, refusing to budge from his place. We'd plead, beg, and cajole, finally pulling him up by his arms, trying to force him to walk. And then he'd begin to wail. He would look up at me, eyes desperate, and jam his tiny fist into his mouth as if trying to pull out the words that would not come.

One early Sabbath afternoon, my friend was in bed with the flu, so I walked up the steps to Chaim's apartment alone. Chaim's father opened the door, and immediately I knew that something was wrong. It was the plates still filled with food that lay untouched on the empty table. It was the boy, one of Chaim's brothers, crouched in the corner, eyes peering out from behind a chair, his other siblings nowhere to be seen. It was Chaim's father, pale, angry, his head bare, his side curls disheveled, staring at me as if he had no idea who I was or what I was doing there. Suddenly, he turned and walked away without a word. His tzitzit strings swung furiously over his boxers. His bare legs hurried across the living room. I wondered where Chaim's mother was.

Abruptly, he turned and walked back to me as if to say something, and then stopped and returned to the corner of the room near the door, where an infant's glider stood.

"So you're taking Chaim out," he said flatly, looking at me from behind the swing.

"Yes," I said.

He pushed the swing in frustration. We watched the empty seat glide in a silent arc.

"What's the point?" he asked, his words like a jab in the air. "Why take him out?"

For a moment I was quiet. Chaim's father did not wait.

"Do you see anything in him?" he asked. "When you take him out, do you see anything in him? Anything at all?" And he stared at me suspiciously.

"In Chaim?" I asked.

But Chaim's father never heard me.

"What's the point?" he said, fear and rage in his voice. "What's the point? My family keeps telling me to put him away—there are homes for such kids. No one sees anything in him. There's nothing there to see. Only my wife refuses"—he did not seem to notice the crouching child in the corner; he just pushed hard against the swing and went on—"to see reality. We can't fix him. It's hopeless. Enough. My family's behind me. They keep telling me, 'What are you doing to your other children? It's the family or it's the boy—you could barely manage as it is,' and this. This. This. This makes no sense. There's only so long you can drag this out. Why are we dragging it out? I don't see anything. There's nothing there. She's still changing his diapers. He's four years old. He can't talk—not one word. We took him to doctors. The school is useless. If somebody would know what to do, how to make him better...They just know that he's autistic, and now what? She can't care for such a child. He's destroying her. It's destroying this home. We have other children. There's nothing in the boy—nothing. I don't know what she sees. It's the family or it's the boy. It can't be both."

He stopped, his hands hanging limply at his sides, his rage spent. The glider slowed down, coming to a stop.

I looked at the Shabbos table, the pot filled to the brim with the waiting *chulent*. In the rooms around me there were children, I knew, hiding. They were hiding beneath blankets, and inside closets, hands covering ears, breathing very, very quietly, waiting for the battle to end. The wide eyes still stared out at me from behind the chair in the corner.

I could hear the harsh sound, the squeal of the chair as it was shoved back, hitting the counter. I could hear my father stride down the hallway. The front door slammed shut and he was gone. The walls of my room trembled. What if my father left the house and never returned? Would he take me with him? Would I want to go? Would my mother take Nachum and tell the rest of us to leave?

"Say *'baruch!'*"

"Say *'baruch!'*"

"I will buy you a Lego, a flying horse! *Baruch, baruch! Baruch, baruch!* Say *'baruch'!* It means 'blessed'!"

And I told Chaim's father that there was hope. I knew because I had such a brother. Nachum was thirteen months younger than me, I told him, and once he could not speak. He could not even hum a tune like Chaim. But today my brother was fifteen, and we had long conversations. He attended a regular high school, with help. His bar mitzvah had been two years ago and it had been beautiful. He went to shul every day and prayed. My brother could read and write, on a low level, but still, he could read and write. He knew who I was, and who everyone in our family was. He was learning to take the city bus by himself to school. He was autistic, still different, but he looked you in the eye when you spoke.

Chaim's father stared at me as I told him about my brother, about my mother and the things she had done. He was silent until I stopped speaking. I could see his eyes questioning, as if he did not know whether I could be trusted, as if I'd just dangled before him an impossible lie.

He stepped in front of the glider. "I'll tell my wife you're here," he said, and disappeared into the hallway.

A few minutes later, Chaim's mother came out, holding him tightly by the hand. Chaim stared blankly ahead. We spent two hours at the park, where I watched him wandering around, seeking something. Then slowly he began to hum until we went back home.

In the end, I don't know what happened to the boy. I did not find out exactly what had triggered the fight between mother and father. I didn't have to. This was a story I knew.

A few weeks after the incident, Chaim's family moved to a different city and I never heard from them again.

I often wondered about him—not Chaim, but the one behind the chair. I wondered what he felt in that closed-in corner as he listened to me speak. Had he been angry? Relieved? Was he afraid that I had convinced his father to keep the crazy brother? I wondered if he prayed for him to die.

*   *   *

A few years passed. I was twenty years old, newly married, and like thousands of Orthodox couples, my husband and I had moved to the Holy Land, where young newlyweds went to start their lives. For several years I lived in Jerusalem, in an ultraorthodox neighborhood just ten minutes away from my Aunt Itta. It was then that my brother and I grew very close.

At that point, nineteen-year-old Nachum spoke freely and did not stop unless you told him to. He had finished high school and held a paying job at a printing center. During the week, he took lessons in photography and computers, and twice a week he exercised at the local gym. On Fridays he helped my aunt prepare for the Sabbath, and if he had time, he'd come by my house and we'd sit and chat. Sometimes he'd offer to take the baby for a walk.

I watched him from my window one such sunny afternoon, as he carefully pushed the stroller down the hill. It struck me as it did every once in a while, this incredible thing that had happened: I could hand Nachum a bag, a bottle, and my son in his stroller, and trust that he'd know what to do. But just as immediately, the guilt rushed in, pulling tighter and tighter around my chest. I was expecting my second child, and the questions and fears that had plagued me the first time had returned.

The question had occurred to me suddenly, during the third month of my first pregnancy, as I stared down at the contours of my softly swelling body and the growing bump that held my child.

What would I do if my baby was autistic?

I had looked up in shock at the thought.

What would I do if the baby was autistic?

For months, I grappled with the thought. For months, I struggled, because not once could I answer the question: Would I take my own child home?

I could not understand myself. My brother was the miracle boy. Nearly a decade had passed since the book *My Special Brother* was published, twelve years since Mrs. Friedman had reassured me of my brother's higher soul, and within the tightly bound circles of the Orthodox community, attitudes had changed drastically.

Perhaps it was the explosive growth of the community, and the increasing numbers of special children born, making them harder to hide. Perhaps it was the small number of families who had successfully raised such children, now part of the community, each in their own way. Perhaps it was the growing pool of resources, treatments, and experts coming in from the outside world, making it a possible thing to raise such a child. One thing was certain: by the time I graduated high school, there was a growing number of organizations, specialized schools, and programs that helped families cope. There were volunteer groups, often organized through the Orthodox schools, which sent their students to help in such homes. Things were different from the way they were in the world I had grown up in. Now the ultraorthodox truly embraced such children as higher souls. Now few ten-year-olds worried that no one would marry them because of an autistic brother.

So I should have felt different when the possibility struck me that I might have an autistic child. I should have felt the instinct to protect, like my mother's; a willingness to fight, like my aunt's; a deep certainty that this was the direct will of Heaven. But I hadn't felt that. What I felt was terror. Then shock at the terror, and waves of guilt.

It took me years to understand my own guilt, to see that my psyche did not care that the present reality was different; it had reacted to the experience of the past. Because I knew the hell from the inside, the torturous twists and turns of that nightmarish road, the mind-bending exhaustion, the chaos, the stuff that rips families apart. My reaction during my first pregnancy was not that of a mother, but of an eight-year-old child watching her family unravel. My brother's screams still echo in my head. I can still hear the thud of his skull against the table.

I have since learned to stop wrestling with the question of what I would do if I had an autistic child. Instead, I stand in awe of those in my family who finally made it work, because it was in that excruciating confrontation with myself that I also fully absorbed the enormity of what my parents had faced. I understood that they had been forced to choose between one child and the rest of us in a time and place where the two could not be.

Today, I watch my brother going about his life, ever growing, ever changing, at each new stage and development learning to cope with the complexities that will always be his life. I watch him thriving and struggling, part of the first generation of autistic children to survive into adulthood, outlasting every expectation and hope of what such a boy could be.

*　　*　　*

A few years ago, I wrote my first article about my brother. The article, published in an Orthodox magazine based in New York and Israel, was read by my parents, aunts, and cousins, and also by Nachum.

I had not meant for my brother to read it. The article included the blunt description of him, which I had used as a child, as my "crazy brother." But one day on the phone, after complimenting me on the piece, my Aunt Itta's voice filled with tears and emotion. She said, "Nachum is eager to talk with you. He read the article too." And suddenly, he was on the line.

"I, I, I rih-read the article...about me when I was a boy."

I swallowed hard.

"So, so, so—it was—it was vih-very, very nice."

I cringed. "You liked it?"

"Yih-yes," he answered. "But—but. But when you were a little girl—you, you, you—you were also autistic?"

I was silent, baffled by the question.

"Whih, whih-when—when you were a little girl, you—you were also autistic?"

Still silent. Then I said, "Uh. Uh...I can't...I can't remember. I don't think so. I'll ask Ima."

My brother absorbed this.

"I don't, I don't...I don't remember either," he said, followed by a moment of thought. "It's hard to remember."

"It is," I said.

Then firmly, he informed me, "Today. Today. Today, I am not like then. It was something—sih-something from when I was a boy."

I said, "Yes."

"Today, today, today, I am diffehr'ent. I still have pih-roblems—I still have pih-roblems. But, but—not like then."

"I know," I said. "I was writing about the past. A long time ago."

"About the past. About the past. Yes. In the past, I was vih-very autistic. You remember."

"Yes," I said.

"Then—then I didn't talk," he said. "Didn't talk. Now I can talk. I can talk."

I tried to reassure him.

"It was long ago," I said to Nachum. "Today you are almost like me, like everyone."

There was a silence as he pondered this.

"Nih-not like everyone," he said. "I am nih-not like everyone. I have still, I have still specific, sih-psychiatric pih-roblems that obstih-ruct, obstih-ruct, obstih-ruh—that bother me. In the dih-daily routine. Thi-that's why I go to a psychologist, a psychologist. To help me think . . .

"Kacha zeh, kachah zeh," he finished. "It's the way it is."

"It's true," I said.

"Whi-when, when I was a boy," my brother went on, "I was autistic . . . I was vih-very autistic . . . autistic." He repeated himself again and again, as if to better observe himself at that distance. "I, I, I . . . I was autistic. But nih-now I am not like that."

"You are not," I repeated. "You are not like that anymore."

"Nih-now I can talk."

"Right. You can talk."

"Nih-now...now I can remember."

"Now you remember everything."

"Now...nih-now...now we can do things together."

"Now we do things together."

"Nih-now I am just your brother. Your other, crazy bih-rother from Israel."

He chuckled at the memory of that long-ago joke.

"Yes," I said, and nothing more, because what more was there to say? Now he was just my brother, my deeply pondering brother, and I his amazed sister.

About the Author

Judy Brown wrote the controversial novel *Hush*—a finalist for the 2011 Sydney Taylor Book Award for outstanding book on the Jewish experience—under a pseudonym because she feared backlash from the Chassidic world. Brown's identity has since been revealed and she has left Chassidism. She has been profiled in the *New York Times Magazine* and has written for the *Huffington Post* and the *Jewish Daily Forward*. Brown holds a master's degree in creative writing and lives in New York City.